SAVED TO SERVE

To MUMMY HAPPY
16th SPIRITUAL BIRTHDAY

LOVE FROM

JOShua

Rebekah

Timothy

CALEB

&

REUBEN

xoxo xo

SAVED
TO
SERVE

The life story of Wasyl Boltwin

John W. de Silva

JOHN RITCHIE LTD
CHRISTIAN PUBLICATIONS

40 Beansburn, Kilmarnock, Scotland

ISBN 0 946351 96 1

Copyright © 2000 by John Ritchie Ltd.
40 Beansburn, Kilmarnock, Scotland

First Edition 1996; Second Edition 1998; Third Edition 2000

Typeset by John Ritchie Ltd., Kilmarnock
Printed by Bell & Bain Ltd., Glasgow

Acknowledgments

I gratefully acknowledge the help and co-operation of my wife Lydia, of Marg Huxtable, and of Wasyl and his wife Joy; also the editor of this edition, Dr Bert Cargill.

Above all, we acknowledge the graciousness of the Lord, who has given those involved the opportunity and means to complete the task.

AUDIO VERSION: Unabridged audio cassettes of the book have been produced by the CHRISTIAN BLIND MISSION INTERNATIONAL, and are available from their libraries.

Contents

Preface

This volume recounts the life story of Wasyl Boltwin, my father in law, as he related it to me. It is, however, not the first occasion that this story has been published. In 1972, Dr F A Tatford (a former director of the UK Atomic Energy Commission, Christian evangelist and Bible expositor) published a booklet containing an abridged story of the conversion and call of Wasyl, after meeting him in Europe on the mission field. In that booklet he was referred to as Ivan Tomski for security reasons.

Due to this first publication being out of print, and because many have expressed the desire to hear and pass on the testimony of Wasyl, it was decided, according to the Lord's will, to undertake a retelling. This volume presents a more full and detailed account of the events in Wasyl's life, events that raised him from the mire of hopeless atheism, and placed him upon the unmoveable rock of assurance and lasting peace, through faith in the person of Christ. It tells how he was saved to serve.

J. W. de Silva (Victoria, Australia 1998)

Wasyl and Joy 1996

Introduction

The pages of this book tell of events in the life of Wasyl Boltwin, the defining occasion being his conversion to Christianity. It was this event and the circumstances attending it, that committed him to a life in which he would take every opportunity to proclaim Christ and His gospel. And, it was for this cause that he agreed to take me on a journey which began in a little village in Siberia called Belgrad.

This journey will take you, as it took me, to parts of Europe during some of its darkest and most turbulent days under Stalin and Hitler, to post-war England, and to the tranquil repose of a provincial Welsh Bible college. From there, we are taken to mission fields in Europe, some of which lay behind the Iron Curtain, and finally to Australia. Here, a great and effectual door has been opened, enabling Wasyl to take the gospel to hundreds of people living within Australia and also within the liberated frontiers of the former communist bloc countries.

This account is one of victory through Christ amidst deep despair and defeat. Wasyl's early life was indeed one of great hardship, yet, as he readily declared, not so great as that of many who shared those times. His story is related here to encourage believers in Christ, those of the heavenly calling, in their holy faith, and also to serve as an evangel of hope to those who have not yet accepted Jesus Christ as Lord and Saviour.

CHAPTER 1

Left to Die

It has been said that Siberia's hostile climate and sheer isolation make demands on life that could be met only by the hardiest physical and mental constitution. We would be told that within the Siberian theatre, we see an enactment of Darwin's principle of the "survival of the fittest". That is, of course, if we choose to ignore the unerring and gracious intervention of an omniscient God in the affairs of man. To try to interpret the course of Wasyl's life apart from the will of God, whose mercy is in the heavens and whose faithfulness reaches to the clouds[1], is to deny that our times are in His hand[2] and to feed the vain fantasies of humanism.

In August 1925, the people of Belgrad in Siberia were busy making the most of the remaining weeks of summer. Winter would soon cast its icy veil over the land and working in the fields would become impossible. The inhabitants of this region knew better than to disregard the uncompromising agenda installed by nature! Only the very young, aged, infirm, and women in confinement were exempt from the arduous daily routine of labour in the fields.

This was the case with *Ustya*, a gentle matriarch with a robust constitution. While the small army of villagers toiled under the summer sun harvesting gherkins, she was giving birth to Wasyl, her twelfth child. The precise date of his birth and many details of his childhood are unknown. We do know, however, he was one of fourteen children born to Ustya and *Yakob*, and that seven of his siblings had already died, a grim legacy of the harsh Siberian environment. The four remaining children were now joined by Wasyl, another brother, and later a sister *Natasha*.

Wasyl was not expected to live when, nearing the age of three, he, along with many in the village, contracted an illness thought to be typhoid or cholera. Poor nutrition, the harsh climate and lack of any medical aid kept mortality rates high. When an epidemic such as this struck, as it did from time to time, the death rate reached tragic proportions. Many had already died from the current pestilence, on average one from each household.

This was an all too familiar situation for Ustya, who over the years had buried seven of her children. Defying the invading chill of early winter, and cradling Wasyl in her bosom, she undertook a thirty kilometre trek in order to consult a doctor, only to have her fear confirmed. Once again she had done all she could! All manner of potions and her devoted care had proved unsuccessful! One evening, she lifted Wasyl out of his cradle and, in solemn resignation, tenderly placed him in a "secluded" area near the stove so he could die. The rest of the family looked on in grim silence. With forlorn eyes and in a voice mellowed by profound sadness, she instructed the other children that only water could be given to their brother. Scarce provisions could not be spent on those who had no chance of living.

However, sibling love and curiosity knew nothing of this seemingly harsh but pragmatic prohibition. It was, perhaps, only the unscarred hearts of the very young who could believe concerning the very ill, that while there is life, there is hope! So, from time to time, the frail constitution of this ailing boy was secretly sustained with food from his siblings, especially by his eighteen year old brother, *Petro*.

One, two, and three days passed, and Wasyl had not succumbed. His fevers and rigors had subsided. The family now organised a concerted vigil, sustaining him with frequent morsels of food. Slowly he began to revive. His feeble rallies became the focus of the whole family, each member competing to bestow upon him care and affection! To the joy of all, he rallied to the point of managing an occasional stumbling walk. After a few weeks, he recovered fully, but the illness had taken its toll and he was known in the village for some time as the boy who was "sickly".

Such was Wasyl's first and early journey into the valley of the shadow of death, one of many he would make in his lifetime. All have since caused him to bear witness to the gracious rod and staff of the Great and Good Shepherd.

CHAPTER 2

Early Days in Siberia

To understand properly the significance of the many changes in Wasyl's life, and begin to appreciate his resolute commitment to Christ, it was needful, as I discovered, to learn something of the cultural, climatic and political environment which shaped his early life and attitudes.

SIBERIA - the land, its climate and people

Siberia is that vast and virtually unchallenged region that sweeps eastwards of the Ural mountains in the country of Russia. Its varied and often inhospitable landscape is bounded in the north by the frigid Arctic waters, the Pacific Ocean to the east and those slumbering Urals to the west. The ancient oriental regions of Kazakhstan, Mongolia, and China define its southern perimeter. Successive governments regarded Siberia as a place of exile for criminals and dissidents. Its isolation and punitive climate played a significant role in the "rehabilitation" of such persons, among whom were two of Russia's infamous sons, Lenin and Stalin.

Wasyl remembered the distinctive timetable of the seasons, each one bringing its particular demands on life. Winters were very severe, with temperatures between minus 35 and minus 40 degrees celsius, occasionally plummeting to around minus 50 degrees. Snow blanketed the ground for up to five months of the year, often covering the little houses. *Zima* - winter, brought occasions of isolation. Days of incessant blizzards made contact between the families in the village, at times impossible!

Wasyl's house was built by his father and, like other houses in the village, had just one rather incommodious room, with a few small glass windows moulded into the walls. It was basically a "wattle and daub" construction with an earthen floor, a roof of wood and mud and a single fireplace-cum-stove. A narrow corridor linked this room to the barn which housed the livestock during the coldest months. In addition to storing food, the barn sheltered the family's water supply, a well about 25 metres deep.

In winter, the wooden cover of the well was overlaid with several feet of straw to prevent the water from freezing. So effective was this insulation that the water remained tepid. Paradoxically, in summer, with the straw removed, the water was cold!

Life during winter was spent predominantly indoors, which cultivated deep family intimacy and solidarity. Wasyl and his siblings carved wood and used charcoal from the fireplace to make drawings. His mother spent the long cold months making and mending clothes, some of which were made from marijuana stalks. These were harvested and frozen during the previous winter, then beaten into strands for spinning and weaving the following year.

Wasyl's father spent his time doing "man's work", repairing and making shoes and leather garments. Winter shoes were made from wool beaten into a felt texture and overlaid with rubber. They were quite water-proof, but they caused one's feet to sweat terribly! When an animal died or was killed for meat, the skin was beaten and cut to provide outer garments. The hair was retained to provide additional insulation. Families had to innovate, and utilise much of what came to hand in order to keep the creeping cold from invading every vestige of life. Children were taught to improvise and regard all material things as having value, if not for today, then for tomorrow when they might mean the difference between life and death. Wasyl's well known propensity still to keep anything that may be useful bears witness to this acquired frugality.

At nightfall, an eerie silence engulfed the village and surrounding plains. Wasyl would often peer through the small windows looking over the vast reaches of snow, letting his imagination run with the shadows and sounds. There was a sequel melodrama, a nightly pantomime performed by strange dancing shapes on the walls, conjured by flames in the open fireplace, accompanied by the crackle and hiss from burning logs.

On some nights, the rampaging wind howled over the land and entombed the house under a mountainous snow dune. Clearing drifts of snow from the doorway and windows was a daily task performed by Yakob and his sons using wooden shovels. It was gruelling and laborious work.

On a cloudless evening, a fully orbed setting sun transformed the countryside into a wonderland. The snow drifts took on hues of pink, purple, orange and red in a stunning kaleidoscope of colour. When darkness fell, stars like countless jewels sparkled against a sable sky and when the moon was full, it cast a ghostly luminescence across the plains. Frequently, the ethereal silence was pierced by a wolf's howl, a chilling reminder that however serene they appeared, death stalked the winter plains in many forms.

People did travel at night, but only if it was unavoidable, and not without their dogs. Wasyl's family owned three dogs, two huskies and a smaller breed, for protection against wolves and as a deterrent to foxes. On night errands, the villagers took with them bundles of hay which were set alight to ward off ravaging wolf packs. People travelling with horses would be given early warning, because at the first scent of wolves, the horses would come to a dead stop and would continue only after patient coaxing.

There were days, however, when the white tempests abated. Wasyl and the other children were able to sledge in the snow, or skate on the frozen ponds using their homemade wooden skates, making the most of the gentle warmth of the winter sun.

Of all seasons, *vesna* - spring, with its gush of life and festive glory was the happiest. Everyone waited for the first sign of a thaw as the snow relented under a more radiant sun. The landscape was transformed into a network of rapid streams that dismembered the icy mantle which had for so long gripped the earth. In some years, spring arrived late causing severe flooding as the snow melted very quickly with the onset of warmer weather. This flooding would cause considerable damage to land and property, often delaying the sowing of crops and shortening the harvest.

Otherwise, spring was a time of communal regathering for man and beast. Cattle and sheep, intoxicated by the balmy zephyrs, responded in crazy gambols when liberated from their winter seclusion. The lucent grace of each morning was heralded by a rousing chorus from ducks, chickens and geese, as they joined the hordes of hyperactive sparrows in their anthem to spring. The day's end was not without its ritual evensong. At sunset, melodic strains from the balalaika and mandolin teased the still evening air. The villagers would gather for merry-making, often in each others' homes, their beery singing telling of harvests past and the hope of nature's bounties to come. Man and beast unashamedly exploited the liberty bestowed by the season of buds, for with the coming of summer, festivity would have to cease.

Summers were mild and relatively short, but temperatures did rise on occasions to between 30 degrees and 38 degrees celsius. On such days, the two poplar trees in Wasyl's yard would cast welcome shade over the house. Now the plains were patterned with green fields arrayed with wild flowers. The village acreage was transformed into a mosaic of cultivated plots, tended by men accompanied by the women, their heads kerchiefed and their torsos girded with aprons. Indoors, heady bouquets of flowers adorned the walls and mantles, adding a blush of colour to the otherwise pallid interior.

There was little time for Wasyl, his brothers and sisters and friend *Metji,* to play or feast among the lush wild strawberries, for summer was a time of earnest preparation for the next winter. To be ill-prepared would mean great hardship and quite possibly loss of life. There was wood to be cut and stored, crops to be sown, harvested and preserved, repairs made to the house, and protective ditches to be dug around the land.

All able-bodied family members were allotted tasks and were expected to do their share. As they grew older, the children were expected to become jacks-of-all-trades, a necessary skill in those climes, one that served Wasyl well in his later life. Wasyl's main job was to tend the vegetable garden. Neighbours joined forces to ensure the harvest was completed before the coming chill of autumn. The poor fertility of the land meant that always the ground had to be worked hard to yield its meagre bounty.

The people

In Belgrad there were Russians (the dominant group), Ukrainians, Kazakhs (Moslems), and even some people of Serbian and Hungarian origin. Wasyl's parents were Ukrainian. Despite the ethnic diversity, isolation and climatic extremes bred goodwill and cooperative effort among the close knit and intimate community of twenty-five or so families in Belgrad. This interaction, especially his acquired skill in learning several languages, fitted Wasyl well for his later evangelism among various European nationalities. It also gave him a strong community spirit.

Over the next few years, life in the little village of Belgrad continued in much the same pattern as it had done for so long. Season followed season, each one selecting its own hues from nature's rich palette to paint land and sky. However, winds of change were coming that would bring to these hard working, peace loving people a prolonged period of great suffering and discontent. A sinister force was beginning to make its presence felt in the political and economic life of the USSR at this time.

Member of Wasyl's extended family
beside their village home in Siberia (Natasha third left)

CHAPTER 3

Communism: Collective Misery!

In 1924, the year before Wasyl was born, Joseph Stalin became leader of the Communist Party and of the USSR. Lacking whatever moderation that may have been credited to his predecessor Lenin, Stalin pursued his malignant vision for the USSR with violent aggression. The infamy of his political purges and labour camps are well documented. An estimated 17 to 25 million of his opponents were sent to "*lags*" or camps. The horrors of these have been exposed in Alexsandr Solzhenitsyn's *Gulag Archipelago*. The dictatorial reign of this self proclaimed "man of steel"[3] had, as its singular purpose, to co-opt and constrain all aspects of life under the yoke of communist ideology.

Just what this ideology entails is in doubt even among communists. The people in Belgrad had no desire for the ideological debate. The purists, of course, vehemently deny that the social, economic and political programmes of Lenin or Stalin embraced "true" communism. In the late nineteenth century the ideas of *Karl Marx* provided the cradle for communist revolution in Russia. It was during his relatively comfortable exile in Siberia that Lenin spawned his particular version of Marxist ideology. He and Stalin retained the essential Marxian view of a classless society in which all productive resources are centrally and communally controlled. The national product is distributed according to the principle, *'from each according to their abilities to each according to their needs'!* Such a society, Marx postulated, would naturally evolve under the progressive alienation and impoverishment of the people under capitalist exploitation.

If, however, this transition failed to occur, then *"the death pangs of the old society"* must be met by the *"bloody birth of the new.....only one way, revolutionary terrorism!"*[4] *"When our turn comes"*, wrote Marx, *"we shall not make excuses for the terror!"* [5]

Karl Marx's "red terror" became a measure of first resort under Lenin and Stalin. Indeed, it became Stalin's sum and substance during his infamous reign as dictator of the Soviet Union. But then, terror and constraint has been a precept within all communist regimes. Even today the communist regimes of North Korea, Vietnam, Cuba and that monolithic relic of Marxism, China, all sustain their administration through "red terror". The reason is plain. Communism fails where Marxism fails, being founded upon a naive perception of human nature, a gross misinterpretation of history and a denial of conscience toward God.

We need to be reminded, that *"A good man out of the good treasure of his heart bringeth forth that which is good; and an evil man out of the evil treasure of his heart bringeth forth that which is evil: for of the abundance of the heart his mouth speaketh."*[6] It is the heart that conceives the ideology, primes the conscience and sets its course. What dark benighted chambers they must have been that spawned communism, its "red terror" and blighted conscience!

Communism comes to Belgrad

In 1928, the village of Belgrad experienced first hand the oppressive arm of communism, which came in the push to collectivise private property. Private ownership of land and livestock was considered contrary to the national interest. Peasant farmers who owned more than two cows or employed two or more workers were singled out for special attention. They were branded arbitrarily as *kulaks*, landowners who lent money to peasants charging usurious rates of interest. The name kulak, which meant *"fist"*, was now indiscriminately applied to men, women, children and even infants.

The stated aim of the communists was to "liquidate the kulaks as a class". Along with Christians, they became a focus for communist propaganda. In the official press and literature, kulaks were referred to as *"parasites"*, *"vermin"* and *"enemies of the people"*, their children labelled *"bloodsuckers"* or *"kulak bastards"*!

Stalin's programme to exterminate these so called "rich peasants" began with confiscation of their property. They had to choose between going to a labour camp or starvation. Large numbers were dispatched with great scorn and haste to the lags. Through deliberate deprivation, many died of starvation even before they reached the camps. Instances have come to light where these "opponents" were sent to harvest corn and died from starvation while doing so.

Some people migrated to safer regions, others spent months wandering about the land only to starve during winter. This was an unsatisfactory situation as far as the communists were concerned, after all there was a chance, albeit a slim one, that the kulaks may survive. In its craven push for "social cleansing", the government installed a system of internal passports. This anchored those branded as kulaks, and later on other peasants as well, to a specific area. Without property and any means of livelihood they were left to starve. In 1930, this culminated in the "Terror-Famine"[7] which was contrived to starve millions of peasants, particularly those within the southern European region. The government first confiscated all food and property and then placed an embargo on supplies entering each district. The resulting famine was perpetuated over a three year period by a callous addiction to communist ideology. Wasyl's grandparents on both sides of the family were among those who starved to death as a result of this infamous contrivance by the communists. In the south, in addition to exterminating the peasants, the famine was used to quash the rise in Ukrainian nationalism.

By the early 1930's more than fourteen million peasant families had been driven into communes. Collectivisation and heavy handed enforcement brought unrest and vigorous opposition from peasant farmers. In response to this wide-spread resistance, the government deployed the military and a force known as the "political police"[8]. In the case of the poorer peasants also, private property not confiscated was taxed. If the peasants managed to pay the tax, the rate of impost was increased and continued to increase until the owner was in debt to the government. Peasants who resisted were branded as bourgeois and traitors to communism, and were either killed or deported to the camps to be "re-educated". One way or another, people were forced onto collective farms. They were confused and angry!

Prior to communism, although peasant life was arduous, the people had a measure of security in their own possessions, in their own toil and in the pervading spirit of pastoral fraternity. Collectivisation represented an impersonal system, one that denied self motivation and family fellowship. Most of all, these proud and resolutely independent communities resented not being given the choice between private and communist enterprise. Life was now not only arduous but lived in terror.

Owning three cows was enough to classify Wasyl's father as a kulak and the children as kulak bastards. Their cows were to be handed over to the officials and consigned to a collective farm. The family's future seemed grim. What could be done to avert this? How could they escape the inevitable destiny of those branded as kulaks? Moreover, the health and financial security of this family of nine depended very much on these three cows.

Many farmers throughout the USSR had slaughtered their livestock rather than give them up. At one stage, nearly one half of the country's cattle had been killed and so it became a criminal offence to kill any livestock without written permission from the government. Wasyl's family adopted another ploy. His elder brother expediently took a wife, who then took ownership of one cow. The second cow was gifted to a sister.

The local Party officials were furious, to say the least, when they came to hear of this. All around them people were finding ways to thwart their efforts. Then, one day, the officials and police burst into Wasyl's home. While shouting abuse, they confiscated precious food, tables, chairs and various utensils. So thorough was their pillaging, that Wasyl remembered his mother's loud and defiant rebuke to them - *"We have nothing left for you to take. Do you want to take our children also? "*

Seething with anger, the officials departed, but not before a parting display of vindictiveness. To compensate for the cows, Wasyl's family had to pay a levy to the local Party authority. This was an inhumane impost since it involved payment of food. Generally, farms produced just enough for their own needs, any surplus being used to barter for necessities, such as medicines and clothing, in the towns. This tax meant insurmountable hardship for the family. The officials knew this very well and it was part of the deliberate tactic to force Wasyl's father onto a collective farm. If they could strip him of his self sufficiency and quash his stubbornness, then he would work on a collective. The alternative was to watch his family starve in Belgrad, or die on the way to a lag.

There were vast numbers of peasant families throughout the country in similar straits. Railway sidings were crowded with men (many of whom had been beaten) and their families waiting for cattle trucks to ship them off to the lags.

Escape to Stalinabad

At that time a number of "refugee camps" arose in regions where the oppressive edicts of Stalin were not rigorously enforced. This was, in part, because of their distance from Moscow and, in part, due to their opposition

Wasyl's father Yakob: circa 1930

to communism because of their ethnic identity and entrenched religion.

Wasyl's father decided that the family would flee to a refugee camp in *Stalinabad*, which was about fifty to sixty kilometres north of the Afghanistan border. Stalinabad was

27

in the republic of *Tajikistan* the home of the *Tajiks*, descendants of the Iranians who were once part of the Persian Empire. There they would try to regain their independence and escape the terror of the lags. After selling their few remaining non-essential possessions, they prepared to leave the little village which had been their home for many years. This was not an easy decision. Apart from the waiting uncertainties, they were at risk of being apprehended by the police and punished severely.

Their covert journey involved spending hours on exposed station platforms and travelling in cold train carriages. They had to wait three weeks at *Tashkent* in *Uzbekistan*, a transit stop, before getting seats on the train to Stalinabad. The family were among hundreds fleeing the malevolent regime. Food and shelter were limited, but they made do by careful rationing.

Days later they arrived at the camp only to find their possessions had been stolen from the luggage car. Food, personal papers and clothes were gone! All they had left were the clothes and the little money they had on their persons. Their luggage was insured for three hundred roubles, but the authorities paid only three! As refugees, they were in no position to argue. In all, it was a most deflating beginning to a new life.

Yakob, being a skilled blacksmith and a jack-of-all-trades, soon found a well paying job. No one asked where they were from or who they were, as this was a Moslem region and communism had made few inroads here!

However, their stay in Stalinabad lasted for only about twelve months. The hot, oppressive climate, Yakob's failing health, and malaria endemic to the region, meant moving north. Furthermore, Stalinabad was no longer a refuge from communism. The people of Tajikistan and the surrounding Moslem regions were losing their guerrilla warfare against the might of the Soviet Union. By the time Wasyl's family had left Stalinabad, Tajikistan had capitulated and become a union republic.

A letter of support from a local doctor substantiated their request to leave. They were given permission to return to Belgrad, provided they work on a collective farm. They had little choice, communism was taking a stronger hold and working on a collective was inevitable. At least in Belgrad they would be among familiar surroundings. The unpleasant alternative was to flee to China, which was about five hundred kilometres away over inhospitable mountainous country, the haunt of predacious bandits.

Return to Belgrad - Life on a Collective Farm

The local school

The family now lived and worked on a collective farm. Wasyl resumed formal education, attending a school comprising about one hundred pupils of varying ages. There was only one teacher and the students were divided into two groups. The first group had their classes in the morning for four hours, after which they would be dismissed, allowing the second group their four hours in the afternoon. Free mornings and afternoons were for homework, but little was done as there was always work to do on the collective farm.

To the passer-by, there was nothing unusual about the school. However, schools were a vital instrument in the orchestration of communist propaganda. It was not just a case of promoting the ideals of communism and vehemently denigrating opposing beliefs. Schools were an important part of the "informant" network, where children were encouraged to report people who held beliefs contrary to communist principles. Subtle questions about habits of prayer or religious conversations at home, had led to children unwittingly betraying their parents and grandparents, who were taken away for re-education.

The teacher, who was a Party member, began each session with a vigorous denial of all ideology other than that espoused by Stalin. Impious anti-religious posters were hung on the walls. Religious books, or those containing any deferential reference to religion, were destroyed and replaced by texts compelling atheism. Wasyl and the other pupils were fed a daily diet of anti-religious doctrine. *"Only the old and stupid believe in God!"* *"God does not exist."* And then there was always the threat, *"Those that believe in God are subversive, they are enemies of communism, they must be 're-educated'."* Religion, the *opiate of the masses* and Christianity in particular, was often the subject of official vilification, based on the premise that, *"the rule of Capital will never be extinguished until the last capitalist, nobleman, Christian and officer draws his last breath!"*[9] Church property was initially heavily taxed and then confiscated. Many church buildings and monasteries were destroyed in fits of mindless anarchy. Priests who resisted re-education were imprisoned or put to death. Some were recruited as informers.

Stalin's programme of militant atheism was never going to be successful, for it rejected the basis of good government, that *"The fear of the Lord is the beginning of wisdom"*[10]. Instead, it was a platform of an administration based on the fear of man, a regime of a man of whom it can be said, *"..... that there is no fear of God before his eyes. For he flattereth himself in his own eyes, until his iniquity be found to be hateful"*. It is righteousness that exalts a nation![11]

Indeed, when the fear of God is abandoned by governments, it inevitably manifests itself in immoral administration. The reign of men like Stalin, who "devise mischief upon their beds and abhor no evil", are driven by a base conscience, their souls enslaved by irreverence, their eyes, ears and hands ready ministers of terror!

In his "Manifesto" Marx averred that the idea of God, the idea of immortality, the notion of conscience and the practice of religion must be eradicated. The product of such iniquitous and inebriated thought can be seen in the quill and sword of men like Lenin, Stalin, and latter day disciples of communism. Man becomes a hollow vessel, a receptive host to the base doctrines of humanism!

Humanism patronised a new fashion - rational criticism. Christianity became a prime target of the rational critic, but even their progenitors had to confess, *"whatever else may be taken away from us by rational criticism, Christ is still left."*[12] As the Roman procurator Pontius Pilate found, so they too realised that *no fault can be found in this Man!* It is Christ, His moral perfection and virtue in deed that trouble the rationalist and the communist, for, as Strauss had to confess, *"Among the personages to whom mankind is indebted for the perfecting of its moral consciousness, Jesus occupies at any rate the highest place."*[13] Christianity springs from the purest of hearts and, in consequence, exhorts the purest in thought and in deed. Thus it stood as a troublesome stumbling block to men such as Marx, Lenin, Stalin, and their disciples, pointing an accusing finger to the reason and realms of these proponents and exponents.

It is Christianity with its unique articles of faith, we should note, and not Islam, Buddhism or some other religion, that so vexes the totalitarian communist heart and mind. We know that the *"law was given by Moses, but grace and truth came by Jesus Christ."*[14] The law according to some may be expediently dismissed as the outcome of cultural or ethnic evolution. Grace and truth however, challenge the conscience of all persons and are found to be an anathema to many. These two tenets of Christianity, grace (the bestowal of undeserved goodness), and truth (the eternal verities concerning the matter of sin, righteousness and of divine judgment), have to be quashed and expunged. For what reason? - none except that they run counter to the natural mind cultivated by the code of evolution, that only the fittest should survive and anything which secures physical survival is righteous!

Preoccupation with something that was supposed to be stupid and irrelevant made Wasyl, and he was sure many others, question the motives of the officials. *"What is the harm if people believe in something that is useless? Why spend so much time and effort fighting a god who does not exist?"* However, expressing such views in public or even behind closed doors was dangerous. It was not unusual for informers to report "indiscretions" committed by their own family to Party officials. Great discretion was required on the collective farms as informers were always present, recruited by Party officials, some through voluntary zeal, others through blackmail. To be reported, all you had to do was make a disparaging comment concerning the harvest, such as that the vegetables were too small, express doubts concerning the Five Year Plan, or fail to attend propaganda meetings held in the village.

Wasyl noted that many people in the village had disappeared. It was common to wake in the morning to find friends had vanished. They were always taken at night by the political police (referred to as "black birds" or "ravens"), after they had been reported for some trivial or concocted statement against the government. Desperate relatives and friends would plead for information concerning their fate, but they were met with arrogant silence from the authorities[15]. The whole system was coordinated by fear and suspicion, which added to the economic repression of people on the collectives. Wasyl was content to remain a passive atheist!

Farm economics

Most of the produce from the collective was paid to the government in exchange for raw materials and equipment. The amount paid was fixed, therefore it did not reduce in times of poor harvest. The remaining output was distributed among the farm workers according to the number of "days of labour" they had earned.

Yakob and the other workers were paid as follows. All

tasks on the farm were valued in terms of days of labour. For example, ploughing one hectare of land could be valued at, say, one day's labour; ploughing two hectares could be worth two days' labour.

At the end of the production year - September/October - the number of labour days Yakob had worked was totalled. Labour days would then be exchanged for the *residual* farm produce at a fixed rate. For example, two kilograms of flour could be valued at, say, ten days' labour. These exchange rates were not determined until the end of the season, causing uncertainty as to how much produce would be earned by each worker. Further, the farm produce received was the total allotment for the following year, necessitating scrupulous daily rationing. This is why Ustya, and all who had charge of the household larder, placed it under lock and key. With possession of the larder key went the responsibility for the family's food supply and the family's survival during the next winter.

Wasyl and his siblings often wanted another piece of bread as a result of having expended extra energy or just because they were growing children. His siblings were more forward than Wasyl and often asked for extra food. Their mother's stock answer was, *"If I give you extra today, there will be less for you tomorrow!"*

Wasyl could not remember a time when food was adequate or of great variety. Prior to communism, breakfast and dinner throughout the year consisted mainly of borscht - a soup comprising potato and cabbage or bean and pumpkin, served with bread (butter was rare). Occasionally in summer a sheep or pig was killed to provide meat, supplemented by one of their doves (a delicacy) or a snared rabbit. Any remaining meat was salted for winter. There were no such "luxuries" on the collectives where they now were.

Beside where they now were, working on the farm, Wasyl's father had been given a job in one of the Machine-Tractor-Stations (MTS). These complexes housed and serviced all farm equipment used by the collectives. Each collective farm had to contract with the MTS for equipment needed for large scale cultivation. This was another way in which collectives were centrally controlled.

There were benefits in working in a MTS. You were paid in roubles, which enabled provisions to be purchased in the towns. You were also given a travel permit, albeit a restricted one. Travelling beyond designated areas was prohibited; to be caught meant severe penalties and even a charge of subversion.

These benefits did not compensate for the dour and impersonal life on the collective farms. Some workers believed the endless propaganda; their allegiance was rewarded by certificates of merit and medallions. Many however, pined deeply the loss of individuality and the denial of self motivation. Sadly, men sought solace in vodka, and many, including Wasyl's father, became hopeless alcoholics. Wasyl, too, when a young man, was given to times of intemperance! The endemic alcoholism within the Soviet region bears grim witness to the dehumanising ideology of communism.

Wasyl's father, then in his sixties, had to walk a round trip of fourteen kilometres to the MTS and, given his age, his alcoholism and the cold, this work soon became impossible.

The flight to the Caucasus

In 1939, Yakob and Ustya decided to risk travelling without permits and relocate the family in a region within the old silk route, the eastern perimeter of the Black Sea called the Caucasus. There the climate was milder and living standards reputedly higher. Perennial snow-capped mountains, high valleys and verdant fertile plains inter-laced by fast flowing rivers typified the region. Many of the inhabitants of the area could trace their origins to the Hellenistic, Roman, Byzantine and Persian dynasties.

One evening after arriving home from the MTS, Yakob

packed a bundle of provisions, and at dawn the next day he took Wasyl, now aged fourteen, and left for the Caucasus. The plan was that once settled he would set about bringing the rest of the family there also.

Their journey began with a seven kilometre walk to the main road through the still grey dawn. The early morning air was cold even though spring had arrived. The slush created by the melting snow made walking difficult and quite unpleasant, even the main road was a quagmire. After several minutes a truck appeared, labouring noisily through the mud. The offer of money to the driver secured them a ride. Yakob was going to need most of the roubles he had with him to bribe people all along the way.

After a meandering and lurching three-hour journey over sixty kilometres, they arrived at the nearest railway station, one of many transit stops with little shelter or other amenity. Getting tickets without a proper permit and without pre-arrangement was going to be tricky. However, paying around 250 roubles in bribes for tickets costing 150 roubles bought them two seats on a train to *Omsk*, about five hundred kilometres away.

Late the next day, they arrived at Omsk, a place of great significance for two reasons. Firstly, they were now relatively safe since the regulations here were more liberal than in Belgrad. Secondly, it was here that Wasyl had his first taste of white bread!

After another arduous train journey throughout which Wasyl and his father slept, they arrived in the Caucasus. Once again, Yakob was able to get a job on a collective farm as a blacksmith, and began to make plans to reunite the family. This process was to be a slow and delicate one!

Some months later, the collective overseer finally agreed to help bring the rest of the family to the Caucasus to work on the farm. His efforts were only partially successful. Wasyl's elder brother and sister were refused permits; they were declared to be "indispensable" to the collective farm in Belgrad. The family separation was cause for great distress. It would have been much greater had they known they would never meet again.

Despite the abiding sadness brought by the separation, they resigned themselves to the routine of life on this new collective farm. It was much safer this way, as Stalin's sinister terror still stalked the land. However, other winds of change were again to usher in events that would alter their lives profoundly. These events were already re-shaping the political and economic structure of Europe. They would yet plunge Wasyl into a deep vortex of uncertainty, fear and despair, to the extent that he would even take steps to end his own life.

CHAPTER 4

War: Despair and Deliverance

To date, Wasyl's life was untouched by the great war raging in Europe. The USSR initially had no quarrel with the Third Reich and its conquest of Poland and Czechoslovakia. However, the fall of France in 1940 and the prospect of Britain capitulating, caused concern within the Soviet Union over the eventual balance of power in Europe. It was left to Adolf Hitler to precipitate conflict between Germany and the USSR. His voracious appetite for power fuelled by his megalomania, saw the USSR become part of his territorial ambitions. In June 1941, Hitler's military machine invaded the Soviet Union and with relative ease seized large areas of the Ukraine and White Russia.

Whereas communism preached equality within a classless society, the overriding political, economic and social objective of Hitler's National Socialism, was to contrive and promote racial inequality. Hitler and his hysterical propagandists cultivated within Germany and Austria general acceptance of the idea of Aryan physical and intellectual superiority.   The new order was to ensure that economic and political power resided exclusively in the hands of the elite Aryan race - the 'purest of blood'! According to Hitler, the downfall of nations is the result of racial impurity. Inferior races such as the Slavs and the Jews were to be isolated and subjugated. In the case of the latter, subjugation soon meant extermination under the Third Reich's heinous "final solution", which really was designed to exterminate all Jews within central and eastern Europe.

His hatred for the Jew also meant antipathy towards Christianity, insofar as it was regarded as an extension of Judaism. The Christian doctrine had to be moulded to accommodate the notion of racial purity, the Old Testament was to be discredited and discarded.

Stalin had his lags and the NKVD, Hitler had his concentration camps and the SS, or Nazi secret police. Their task was to establish and maintain conscience and creed according to the doctrine of National Socialism within Germany and within countries subjugated by Germany.

The initial invasion into Soviet territory by the armies of the Third Reich was very successful. Two years after they had moved to the Caucasus, Wasyl's family was living under German occupation. German rule brought mixed blessings to the people. On the one hand they were free to resume religious activities, churches were reopened and services convened for christenings and celebration of Mass. But this was of no benefit to Wasyl's family as they were not religious.

At first, the people welcomed German occupation, as it meant an end to communist rule and they greeted the occupying forces with traditional offerings of bread and salt. However, once entrenched, the Germans began persecuting the Slavs whom they regarded as "sub-humans". Also, summary execution was the order of the day. For every German killed by the resistance, one hundred local inhabitants would be shot. Such an execution had taken place in a neighbouring village and it was enough to cause fear and hatred amongst the local people towards the Germans.

As time passed, the German presence in the Caucasus appeared to diminish. In January 1943, to the great surprise of the villagers, the Germans withdrew from the immediate area. They thought it must have had something to do with a ferocious battle some thirty kilometres away the previous day. Of even greater amazement was the sight of a Russian trooper, shouting as he rode through the village.

"All males must report to the centre of the village!"
"You are required to report now!"
"All males go to the village centre!"
"Go now!"
Astonishment soon gave way to terrible, cold reality!

Was this a call for men in the village to go to the front? They had heard of the terrible carnage taking place at the front lines. Was it now time for their sons, fathers, grandfathers, uncles and brothers also to go? A sombre air enveloped the village as men began to move in silent apprehension to the place of muster.

They came from all directions, filing through the snow-bound streets. As they came together, the sound of anxious conversation increased. *"What is happening, what is this about?"* *"Why do they want us to gather?"* There were many questions and much speculation, but only the youngest were truly ignorant of the reason behind the call of the Cossack. Wasyl, now aged seventeen, knew only too well the reason for the call, for this was not the first time he had been summoned to a muster. During the autumn of 1941 and the spring of 1942, he and many others, women included, were conscripted to dig large ditches to try to thwart the German advance.

Well, he thought, this surely could not be a call to dig ditches since this was already winter. They did not have to wait long before being addressed by an official from the NKVD, *"Comrades, you are required at the front to defend the Motherland from the black tide of German evil. It will be your privilege to serve with your brave comrades in arms for the glory of the Red Army and our leader Joseph Stalin."* These fearful words had little time to sink in before the men were being selected and grouped according to "battle tasks" - artillery, machine guns, rifles, etc. Wasyl was appointed to a machine gun group.

But more trauma was in store, for the official declared dispassionately, *"We cannot supply you with any guns or ammunition, supplies are 'temporarily' unavailable.*

You will receive them later, along with your army uniforms."

Upon hearing this, the men at first stood in stunned silence, then in an angry, spontaneous protest they shouted, *"Niet niet!"* *"Impossible, ridiculous! How do you expect us to protect ourselves, let alone kill the Germans?"* *"What you are expecting us to do is sheer madness."* Their angry objections continued for several minutes. When he had heard enough, the NKVD official launched into a passionate speech, speaking again of the glory of communism, the blackness of fascism and loyalty to Stalin and the Motherland! But the protests, now tainted with sarcasm, continued, *"How can you expect us to defend the Motherland and kill for the glory of Stalin without weapons?"* *"Can you turn snowballs into bullets?"*

The official had heard enough and raised his hands, whereupon the armed guards moved toward the men menacingly. He shouted an ultimatum, *"Be shot here and now as fascist sympathisers and enemies of the Soviet Union, or take your chance fighting the Germans. Get your weapons from Fritz!"* They had no choice, Stalin's henchmen had already proved their readiness to kill their own people for the communist cause.

Just before they left for the front, there was a delivery of some rifles. These were hopelessly unsuited for modern warfare, and in quantity, sufficient only for one between twenty men.

Wasyl's group, about thirty-six in all, marched virtually unarmed towards the German lines. These were not trained militia spirited by communist doctrine, ready to die for the Cause. They were farmers, frail men and young schoolboys! Yes, they would all fight, not for Stalin or communism, but for self preservation, to safeguard their families from the Germans and from communist reprisals.

The extreme cold, the biting wind and sleet made each step a challenge. Ungloved hands meant frozen fingers; poor footwear led to frostbite among many. There was little food, just some stale boiled vegetables. The harsh winter conditions were as much a force to be reckoned with as were the Germans. The only consolation, a small one, was that the cold was not a respecter of persons.

It was not long before they encountered the enemy. German snipers had seen them and began firing. "Behat, behat" (run, run) his comrades yelled. The local men were picked off as they scrambled for their lives in the deep snow, the older ones easy targets for the Germans. Without weapons, they could not offer any defence, let alone mount an offensive. Men lay dead, wounded and dying in the snow. Confusion reigned as they were caught in a crossfire. At the end of the ambush about twenty-six of the company had been killed. They could not advance, neither could they retreat, for fear of the NKVD. Another attack would see them all killed.

No one had told them to expect German snipers hidden in the brush and trees. This appalling situation simply added to their misery. The Red Army was ill prepared and poorly equipped. Stalin's pathological suspicion of those in power around him had led to a purge of the military. Many of the army's battle-hardened and experienced officers had been killed. Morale was low! There were few to give a lead and there was very little military intelligence.

Wasyl and the other survivors hid in freezing February conditions under cover of bracken and in culverts, huddling together for warmth. They fully expected the Germans to come and finish them off. It would have been so easy! Mercifully, they never came. In the morning, a Russian officer accompanied by a few soldiers came along and informed them the snipers had relocated. Fallen comrades lay around them, their frozen faces bearing mute witness to the terror and carnage they had suffered. The survivors instinctively took whatever they needed from the dead. Virtually defenceless, hungry and numb with fear and cold, they moved forward once again, avoiding conflict whenever possible. The places vacated by their fallen comrades were soon filled by recruits from other villages.

It was not until mid-April that they had reason to lift their flagging spirits. A supply of weapons had arrived! Proper food, rifles, machine guns, ammunition and, yes, uniforms (although ill-fitting), all in adequate quantities. However, there was no one to show them how to use these weapons, and to their cost, they had to learn "on-the-job"!

Throughout May to September, Wasyl's machine-gun group was involved in many skirmishes, and experienced many a heavy pounding by German artillery, for which they had no effective answer. He remembered one terrifying session that lasted about eighteen hours, at the end of which walking without treading on corpses and human remains was impossible. The ground was drenched with blood! The army used tractors to move the dead in order to create a path for follow-up troops. During these occasions the question came to him frequently, "Why am I alive while so many have died around me?" Not one conscript from his village had survived except himself.

Captured by the Germans

One day in early October, around dusk, German artillery pounded a large movement of Soviet troops around the town of *Melitopol* in the Ukraine. Wasyl's group was among them. Although the light was fading, the explosion from each shell illuminated the horror around him. His comrades lay dead and dying, twisted and dismembered. Earsplitting, concussive explosions punctuated the constant cries of suffering and shrill commands from officers. He heard the order, *"Stay down and wait for the call to regroup."*

He knew the safest place was the crater made by the last shell. The German artillery methodically spaced their shells about two to three metres either side of the last salvo. With him during this time was an elderly man who fed the machine gun and two younger men who carried the heavy boxes of ammunition. Just where they were he did not know. They may have been caught by a shell explosion or, hopefully, they were safe in a hole nearby. Wasyl jumped into one of the shell craters and dragged his machine gun behind him, hoping the Germans would stick to their routine. They did! The shelling continued all night. He stayed there until midday next day, alone in the crater waiting for the command to regroup.

No command came! Warily he raised his head and looked around. Scores of dead comrades lay all about him. Any who had survived had gone, where he knew not. They must have crept away through the night. He had survived once again! "Why?" he asked himself. Suddenly, he caught sight of two young German soldiers creeping toward him, armed with handguns. They had seen his machine gun and had every intention of capturing it. What was he to do? He had no ammunition. There was no way of preventing the gun from being taken.

Weighty matters of life and death had to be decided upon quickly. He knew that to return to the Russians having lost his machine gun would be considered disloyal. Further, Stalin had declared that Soviet soldiers must fight to the death. To be captured by the Germans by force or through surrender was considered "traitorous to the Motherland"! Suicide not surrender was Stalin's motto! In 1941, Order 270 demanded that Red Army officers who became German prisoners, were to be regarded as "malicious deserters". Their families were to be arrested. In the case of ordinary soldiers, there was the additional decree that their families would be deprived of food rations from the government.

The reality of Stalin's heinous edict had already been patently demonstrated to Wasyl. On one occasion, he was part of a reconnaissance group ordered behind German lines. There they came across a Russian soldier who, like many, had become separated from his unit. He was demonstrably relieved to be found by them and not by the Germans, voicing his joy, "*Comrade, Tovarishch, Tovarishch*", as he embraced and kissed his fellows. However, after returning to camp, despite desperate pleas of innocence, he and a few others in a similar situation were paraded as traitors. This soldier came in for particular vilification just because he happened to speak a little German. A belligerent and conceited commanding officer was going to make an example of them and in so doing parade his loyalty to Stalin. Wasyl and three comrades were selected as observers and charged with telling others of the fate of these and all traitors. But these men were not traitors at all! There in front of Wasyl and the others, these unfortunate men became victims of Stalin's scourge. They were executed - successively shot in the head at close range.[16] Later, special holding camps were set up within the war zone to interrogate Soviet soldiers who managed to escape from the Germans or who had become separated from their units. Many were convicted of desertion on fabricated or circumstantial evidence and shot!

Wasyl now decided the only way out for him was to surrender, come what may. He slowly raised his hands and rose from the crater, shouting *"Stalin caput, Stalin caput!"* At that moment, Wasyl knew he had become Stalin's enemy. If the Russian army ever caught up with him, he would be summarily executed.

The two Germans seized Wasyl and gave him a sound "roughing-up" before taking him to their camp. Strangely, he somehow expected this and did not hold it against them, being relieved he was not shot immediately. He was then driven to an interrogation centre about five kilometres away. The Germans asked him the usual questions concerning his unit and troop deployment, but he could tell them nothing, for he knew nothing. They did not appear overly upset, perhaps because of his youth and the known disarray within the Russian forces. In fact, he was given some fat and bacon rind to eat. He had lost his food bowl and had to use his hat to contain the welcome food! They kept him there overnight and the next day.

That evening a truck with three wounded Russian prisoners arrived. Wasyl remembered well the experience of one of these men called Ivan. This is what had happened.

After a particular battle, the Germans captured Ivan who was among the few survivors. The wounded were to be sent to a German field hospital. But not all of them! The more seriously wounded men were to be shot!

Ivan had sustained two broken legs and was among those considered to be seriously injured. A German soldier approached to carry out the execution order and raised his rifle to shoot Ivan. He began to plead for his life to be spared. He knew a little German and cried through his tears and pain for his wife and five children.

"Nicht schieen bitte!!"
"Nicht schieen bitte!!"
"Mine Frau, Ich habe funf kinder!!"
"Nicht schieen bitte!!"

His pleading and anguish touched a kindred heart, and his would-be executioner, with his finger curled round the trigger and his eye beading down the barrel, began to cry, for he too had a wife and children. The gun was lowered and the German soldier walked away sobbing. Ivan had been reprieved!

Wasyl was summoned to look after Ivan until a truck came to take the wounded to the hospital. He stayed with him all night, ministering to his needs as best he could. The next morning they parted company. Ivan was taken to the hospital and Wasyl was moved to a prisoner of war field camp.

Attempted escape

Camp conditions were primitive. Coils of barbed wire enclosed an area within a field now deep in mud from the September rain. During the day, the prisoners were sent out to dig trenches. Many who survived the shelling and the battles were now dying from starvation, illness and the cold weather. Their daily ration consisted of boiled potatoes, occasionally an insipid vegetable soup, and one loaf of bread to every six prisoners. The thought of escape was on Wasyl's mind and the prospect of it was discussed among a few comrades.

The others decided that an attempt to escape would be foolish as the camp was too well guarded and, besides, where would they run to? They didn't know where they were, the location of German patrols was unknown, cover was scarce, their food was scant, and they were physically weak. Moreover, the advancing Russian army was also their enemy. Wasyl was disheartened by their decision. As he looked around, he saw his own fate in the eyes of those men dying from starvation and illness. He did not have a healthy constitution himself! Despair now enveloped him to the extent that he dismissed fear and reason. He was going to escape on his own! The plan was simple, conceived in desperation rather than in good sense. He knew that there was a section of the barbed wire that was relatively thin and loosely laid. He would wait until nightfall and make his way there. Then, if his timing was right, he could run to a small outcrop of trees. Once there, he would consider his next move.

After curfew, keeping himself low to the ground, he crept to the place he knew along the wire fence. There he crouched, heart pounding and mind racing. He saw his chance and set off, his whole attention fixed on the trees. But as he ran, he noticed how much further they were than he had expected. Too far in fact! The searchlight had turned and he was caught in its full glare. There he stood, illuminated in the still night, trembling with fear and exhaustion, expecting any second to hear the stacatto clatter of gunfire.

Instead, the stillness was broken by shouts from the guards who ran up and quickly secured him. He was then dragged to the main gate. They were furious, and were going to shoot him immediately as an example to other would-be escapers. A rifle was raised to Wasyl's head. All this was happening too fast. The reality of impending death froze all his senses, save fear itself! *"I am going to die now?"* he thought.

Suddenly, an officer arrived and pushed the barrel away. This action caused the bullet meant for Wasyl to fire into the ground! A strained conversation followed between the officer and the guards. Wasyl stood trembling with fear as his fate was being debated, his gaze fixed on the ground at his feet. Then, the officer approached Wasyl and said sternly, *"This time you will not be shot, although the guards are under orders to shoot any prisoner escaping. If you try escaping again, there will be no reprieve."* Wasyl looked up at the officer. He thought he saw tears in his eyes. Perhaps he had a son Wasyl's age, or he had just seen enough of death and despair. Wasyl had been saved yet again!

Escape

The prisoners continued to succumb to starvation and sickness. The approaching winter would make survival all the harder. Escaping was still on Wasyl's mind even though it seemed impossible. The Germans were now alerted and there were fewer prisoners, making supervision easier.

The prisoners knew very little of the war outside the camp, that is until one autumn night when Russian planes began bombing the area. These raids continued for the next few days, causing the Germans to shift the prisoners further behind their own lines. However, even this location came under attack. The Russians were making steady progress. One night, the bombing was virtually over the camp. The first wave of incendiaries illuminated the sky. The Germans took cover as follow-up waves of bombs fell all around. Wasyl now took his chance. He found his way through a gap in the wire fence and ran until he could run no more. Eventually collapsing among scrub in a wood, he fell asleep.

Restlessness and discomfort made sleeping difficult. He got up tired and very hungry. He had no idea where he was. He started to walk and soon came upon farmland. Hearing gunfire, he realised he was still very much within the battle zone. A large pile of hay in a field offered security and warmth. Crawling beneath it, he remained there for a few hours. However, the urge to flee was overwhelming and he decided once again to leave his sanctuary. Looking upward, he saw the gleam of the rising sun. He decided to go in the opposite direction for, in so doing, there would be less chance of meeting up with the Germans retreating to the west and he would keep ahead of the main Russian army advancing from the east.

The whip

It was now late autumn, the wild cherry trees had all but lost their leaves. Wasyl continued to make his weary way westward through the Ukraine. Distance, time and destiny were all unknown, his steps were slow and measured from hunger and fatigue. The mottled golden glory of the season found no response in his soul, save as a harbinger of the coming deprivations of another winter.

Along the forest road ahead he spied a horse whip partially hidden by a thin blanket of autumn leaves. He felt a compulsion to pick it up. Foolishness he thought! If it was a bundle of clothes or, better still, some food, then yes! But a whip? What use would that be? But the feeling persisted to such an extent that he did pick it up and continued walking.

As he rounded a corner, he stopped dead in his tracks.

Fear surged through every nerve in his body. A German soldier appeared out of the trees. *"Halt!"* he shouted. *"I am finished now,"* thought Wasyl. *"I will be shot as a spy!"*

But, to his surprise, the soldier beckoned him on, shouting, *"Boy, your horse and cart are a little way up the road, go and join them. Be quick now!"* He had taken Wasyl to be one of the captured Russian boy-soldiers operating supply carts for the Germans. Wasyl hurried past the soldier, looking neither to left nor right. Once out of sight he quickly ran into the trees, then onto a field where he sought refuge once again under a hay stack. Exhausted, he fell sound asleep!

The sound of sobbing disturbed him. He awoke to see a woman bending over him, her eyes glazed with tears. She asked softly through her sobs, *"Are you hurt?"* *"Are you well?"* *"What is wrong with you......?"* He must have looked emaciated since it had been many days since he had had any proper food or rest. She stared benignly at Wasyl and said, *"Somewhere in the war there is my son. I will do for you what I would hope someone would do for him if they found him like you."*

He made several feeble efforts to stand. Each time he blacked out. She offered to carry him, but he was too embarrassed. She wanted to go for help, but Wasyl protested as this could be too dangerous. Once again he tried to stand, but to no avail. In the end, after resting, he was able to regain his feet, but only with the help of the woman. With Wasyl supported by her ample bulk, they stumbled slowly across the fields to her cottage.

Entering the cottage she led him to a large wooden table. *"Sit here,"* she said, pulling out a chair and easing him down. *"Now I will give you something to eat and soon you will feel better."* She went to the larder, and took out some black bread and a jug of milk. Wasyl eagerly began tucking into the food. Suddenly, the cottage door opened and a man entered the room. He stared at Wasyl for several seconds. Turning towards the old lady, he reached over and snatched away the food shouting, *"What are you doing? He should not be given all this to eat!"* Wasyl was alarmed at such apparent hostility! Who was this unkind man! Even the Germans gave him food! Wasyl sat in silence, too alarmed to chew or swallow. But it was not what it seemed to be.

The man was her husband. He turned to Wasyl and said, *"Son, you are on the edge of starvation. If you eat all this food now, your stomach will become bloated and your insides will twist. You must eat only after you have had some milk, but only half a cup every twenty minutes. You are welcome to stay with us for a while."* Wasyl was so relieved. He gladly accepted the invitation to stay with them for a few days to regain his lost strength.

Several days passed. He relished the warm fire at night, the wholesome food he was given, and the conversation with these kind people.

One evening, the husband rushed into the cottage shouting, *"Wasyl, you must leave, the Russians are close and the Germans are taking hostages as insurance."* The couple had given him civilian clothes consisting of a hat, a heavy coat and a warm shirt. He retained his army pants and boots because they were heavy duty, necessary for the cold. So he bade farewell to his kind friends and set off in his new attire. Tucked under his arm was a small package of food that they had generously given him.

His flight continued westwards, bringing him into areas of thick forest. Land mines were a real danger as the retreating Germans had mined forest tracks, roads, and even fields. He met several people along the way who were able and willing to inform him of the location of German and Russian troops. Many assisted him with food and shelter. It was now November and the cold wind signalled the onset of winter. He had become a professional beggar and had also acquired a certain cunning. How he had changed from the retiring boy who was too shy to ask his mother for food! But one thing he did not do when fleeing was to steal. The risk of getting caught was too high and he would be severely punished.

About a week had passed since he left the elderly couple. A village lay ahead, one that had been recommended by a passer-by as a safe haven. As he came over a rise near the village, he noticed an unusual number of people in the streets. Instinctively, he altered course and approached through a wood. Just then, a mounted German trooper came galloping towards him shouting menacingly, *"You there! Get to the village quickly!"* The German watched as Wasyl hastily obeyed.

Once there, Wasyl discovered the reason for the commotion. The retreating Germans were taking male hostages! He was herded together with prisoners of war and male civilians to be taken behind their lines. After the muster, they were marched to another village about ten kilometres away where they would spend the night before moving on. Upon arrival, Wasyl and the other hostages, were escorted to a field just outside the village. He noticed that in the field were numerous large haystacks.

Although he was tired, the night was not for sleeping! As the others slept, Wasyl was planning to escape. Once behind their lines who knows what the Germans would do? Escape would be very difficult especially in winter. Furthermore, there were reports of retaliatory executions of Russian POWs by the Germans.

There was no way out of the field without passing the armed guards, so during the night he buried himself under as much hay as possible. There he lay until the morning hoping the guards would not miss him, as there were quite a number of hostages sleeping in the field.

The morning call was shouted out, *"Rous! rous!"* Wasyl lay still. He heard shouts and garbled conversation as drowsy and apprehensive men grudgingly awoke to a dawn of uncertainty. Once assembled, they were encircled by the guards. Unbeknown to Wasyl, their usual practice was to burn the hay in order to flush out prisoners as well as to deprive the Russian troops of anything that might assist their advance.

On this occasion it was not to be. Instead the guards began shooting into the hay stacks. Wasyl lay paralysed with fear. This was unexpected! His life rushed before him. For the first time in his life, he began praying, *"God, if you exist please spare me. If I am spared I will spend the rest of my life telling other people that you exist!"* He heard the crack of pistols and the muffled "thump" as bullets passed through the hay all around him. It seemed an eternity. Wasyl kept praying to God to protect him. He had often wondered about God in the past, in a philosophical manner. Now it was a matter of life and death!

The firing stopped as suddenly as it had begun. He was still alive! God had spared him! He was still paralysed with fear. Seconds passed which seemed like minutes. Yet all was quiet! Suddenly, his fear surged to new heights. They had not finished yet! Perhaps they had counted the hostages and knew one was still missing!

They approached the area again, but this time they began randomly piercing the hay with their bayonets. Wasyl virtually stopped breathing as a German stood above him. Had God saved him? He prayed silently again and again, *"God please save me!"* A bayonet struck through the hay, just passing Wasyl's left arm which was welded to his body with fright. Seconds later, he felt another thrust, this time just missing his right side. He grimaced in fear, waiting for the one that would find the centre. Instead, he felt the German stepping aside to continue stabbing the hay next to him. Soon all was quiet!

Two, perhaps three harrowing hours now passed - who knows, time was irrelevant! Nothing! Should he take a look? What if they had posted a guard? Wasyl cautiously pushed his head through the hay. To his great relief, there were no guards, only two children playing several metres away. It was a definite sign that the Germans had gone. And all thoughts of God ended!

He quickly made for the nearby village, taking care to be discreet. There was no sign of soldiers anywhere, The prisoners and the Germans had left. The people in the village fed and housed him for a few days. They told him that the Germans were likely to return and he must move on. But where? The safest direction meant crossing the river Dnieper. The only remaining bridge was forty kilometres away, it would be guarded, and he had no papers to allow him to cross as a civilian.

The couple who had given refuge to Wasyl suggested that he cross at a junction where a "pulley-boat" took people and provisions back and forth across the river. It was decided that the husband would take Wasyl to the crossing and explain the situation. Payment had to be made to be able to cross. Here again, the gracious couple came to Wasyl's assistance and paid the fare.

The next day he was escorted to the boat and he boarded for the crossing. The river was very wide and fast flowing, making progress difficult for the crew. Having reached the other side, Wasyl thanked the men and made his way to the forest, following the many tracks, hoping they would lead to his next meal and another place of refuge.

After walking for several minutes, he had to run into the trees to avoid a German patrol escorting prisoners of war. This necessitated a change in direction. The thick darkness of the forest made it impossible to determine where he was heading. He soon found out! There before him, once again the river Dnieper loomed large and portentous!

He knew he must cross it again somehow. The only way was to swim, so he took off all his clothes and wrapped them into a bundle. With his clothes held high, he slowly stepped in at water's edge. His body rebelled as he sank up to his waist. The icy water and the swift current began to sap his strength. His muscles tightened, his arms and legs ached with the cold. Unable to swim, the swirling current swept him along. He became disoriented and flayed his arms this way and that to try and keep afloat. Fortunately, the unpredictable current took him close to the bank and, in desperation, he managed to cling to some debris rooted along the river's edge. Numb with cold and crippled by cramp, he dragged himself over the icy slush. There he lay, naked, paralysed, cut and bruised! His clothes were gone. There was no one to help. What was he to do now?

As he looked around, to his amazement, he saw his clothes caught in some branches just farther along the edge of the river. After several attempts he was able to rescue them. He wrung the water out of them as much as possible before dressing, then began wandering aimlessly through the forest and snow, often stumbling over the treacherous tracks. He was alone, freezing cold and on the brink of starvation. Despair gripped him! *"Why go on?"* *"Why keep struggling against such impossible conditions?"* *"Who cares if I live or die?"* It was at this point that Wasyl seriously considered taking his own life. He made up his mind to use his belt to hang himself and began looking for a suitable tree.

While trudging through the forest contemplating his suicide, he again came upon the river. He stood and stared in resignation at his watery adversary. If only he could get across! Swimming was now out of the question. He continued to walk and, rounding a bend, he caught sight of a man using a pole to push himself across the water on a raft of logs. The thought of suicide left him as he saw the man abandon the raft and disappear into the forest. Here was a real chance to cross the river and make his way westward again. Wasyl approached the unattended raft cautiously. All was clear, so he jumped aboard and pushed away from the river bank. After an exhausting effort against the current, he reached the opposite bank, by no means however at the intended spot, for he had been swept a few hundred metres down river! No matter, he had crossed and that was the main thing!

He started walking, again following the forest tracks. But then whatever resurgence in spirit he had gained was soon lost. There, coming towards him, were two German soldiers. It was too late to run or hide as they had seen him. *"This is it,"* he thought. *"My luck has finally run out!"* But, to his surprise, they greeted him, one in Russian, the other in Ukrainian. *"Are you hungry?"* they asked, staring at Wasyl's emaciated body. Wasyl thought they were being sarcastic! Perhaps they were, but they were also generous, for they gave him two pieces of dried fish and asked about his state. Wasyl told them of his plight quite freely. Why not? What was there to lose?

To his further great amazement they offered to help him and directed him to another section of the river, a much wider crossing. *"When you get there,"* they said, *"tell the people that Nikita and Peter have given you permission to board the boat. There are hay carts being transported, hide in them. Then go with the people to the collective farm. You must hurry now to get there before curfew or risk being shot."*

Wasyl was buoyed up by both this unexpected offer of help and the meal of fish. He made his way through the forest to the appointed place. It was as the two German soldiers had said, a boat loaded with two hay carts lay moored along the river. He related the message mentioning Nikita and Peter. The crew accepted him without reservation, gave him food and took him to the farm.

Wasyl was uncertain who those two soldiers were, benevolent Germans or Russian soldiers in German uniform? It did not matter, because he was, for the present, relatively safe, warm and had been fed. Why complicate matters with silly questions?

However, Wasyl had learned not to become too comfortable. He knew he could not stay there for any appreciable time, so when he was asked to leave before first light, he was not surprised. He was warned that the

Germans called each morning to collect their allotted milk. Once again he set off into the freezing dawn. It was now winter and the conditions were severe. He hoped that the food they had given him would last until he met his next benefactor.

His nights were spent in culverts, in caves, or under brush that by now was tinted with the white dustings of early snow. Travelling by day was risky, but to travel at night was very dangerous due to the icy pitfalls along the tracks. The last thing he needed was to fall and break a limb; this would mean certain death! Day after day he spent trudging through the cold, battling biting winds and sleet, denying starvation by rationing crusts of stale bread and raw vegetables. The familiar signs of fatigue and a feeling of desperation began to grip him again. If only he could find a place to stay with a little food and some warmth!

He began to think of home as he often did when despair arose within him. How lucky they were back there in Belgrad before the reign of Stalin. Despite the harsh climate and the meagre standard of living they were dry and warm and among those who cared. He wondered what had happened to his family. How he missed them! Would he ever see them again? Where were they? Were they alive? It is certain his brothers had been conscripted and sent to the front. What wouldn't he give for a steaming bowl of borscht around the family fire place!

CHAPTER 5

Survival and Salvation

It was near the end of 1943 now, and for Wasyl these previous months had been so difficult. Unaware of the immense conflict going on farther west in Europe as the Allies and the Nazis struck hard at each other, his only concern was his own survival in the deepening winter in this part of the Ukraine.

The woodcutter

Wasyl had been aimlessly wandering through the forest for three days, when his melancholy reminiscences came to an abrupt stop. He had walked to the forest edge and a clearing lay before him. From the safety of the shadows, he peered across the clearing through the enveloping evening fog. The sound of someone chopping wood caught his ear. Cautiously he crept in that direction, keeping within the perimeter of the forest. There, in a small clearing, a man was cutting firewood.

Wasyl approached him from behind. *"Excuse me sir, can I have some bread, please?"* The startled woodcutter wheeled around and stared at Wasyl in disbelief. *"What....! Who are you? Where did you come from? What are you doing in such a wilderness?"* He stood in silence for several seconds, peering at Wasyl. Then he remembered Wasyl's question. *"I am sorry, I have no bread with me. But if you come to my home I will give you some,"* he said with embarrassment and dismay. He stopped cutting and made two bundles of the wood he had cut. *"Here, you take a bundle. That way if anyone sees us, they will think nothing of it. We must be very careful."*

They walked through the forest, Wasyl following blindly, wondering how much further he would have to carry the wood. No conversation passed between them. Wasyl was glad enough of the silence, as he was exhausted and very cold. He was relieved to see a light shining through the trees ahead. As they drew nearer, he smelt smoke from a wood fire, then the faint outline of a cottage appeared, the light from a window casting its warm glow on the snow-shrouded mantle and walls.

The chance of sitting by a warm fireside, being given food and, who knows, even a dry bed, lifted Wasyl's spirit. His immediate prospects were changing for the better. Little did he know that, shortly, his whole life would soon undergo a profound change!

They reached the cottage and put the wood in a shed. Upon opening the cottage door he was greeted by warmth from the fire and an appetising aroma of onion and vegetable soup. Wasyl found himself in the company of five men, a woman, a little girl and an infant. The woman was preparing dinner while the men, engaged in serious conversation, paused momentarily to nod a greeting to Wasyl.

As they gathered around the fire waiting for dinner, he listened to their conversation. With amazement he noticed that it wholly centred on Jesus Christ. Now, Wasyl had heard the name of Christ spoken often before, but never in such a reverent manner. Jesus Christ was a name he had heard used only when men were cursing, but these men spoke of Him as their Lord.

Their reference to Him as Lord was so apt and it bore an effective and telling witness to Wasyl. May we, who believe in Him, be mindful of the testimony we can bear to others when we call Him Lord. The confession of "Jesus Christ as Lord" marks the beginning of life as a Christian[17], and expresses the divine relationship between Christ and the believer in the new life. May we prize the fact that each time we refer to Jesus as Lord, we glorify God the Father![18] Furthermore, to call Him Lord is to declare that we mean to be governed in all our ways by His Word! Who else but a Christian has the right and obligation to call Him Lord?[19]

Dinner was now ready and bowls were placed neatly along a wooden table covered by a faded cloth. Before partaking, Wasyl was perplexed to see everyone stand with heads bowed and thank the Lord for the food. During the meal the men spoke about a meeting which would be held that night. Wasyl wondered what sort of meeting this was. He dared not ask lest he offend; besides, he was too busy enjoying the bounteous repast! After the meal, thanks was again given to the Lord.

Shortly afterwards, everyone except for Wasyl and the little girl called Mary, donned boots, hats, coats and gloves and left for the meeting. Mary, about thirteen years old, had to stay and put the baby to bed. The diligent and methodical way in which she set about her duties impressed Wasyl. Her bright manner and engaging personality made him relax to the extent that he felt at liberty to question her about the meeting, which baffled him. Who attended it and what was it for? The only meetings he knew about were those held by communists. Why would these people who spoke of their love for Jesus Christ go to a communist meeting, especially within German territory?

So he asked, *"Mary, I heard the men speak about Jesus Christ, but why did they go to a communist meeting?" "Oh no, no,"* she replied. *"These are not communist meetings at all. They are meetings for prayer and Bible study." "A prayer and Bible study! What is this Bible?"* asked Wasyl. Mary tried her best to explain that the Bible is the Word of God. *"But anyone can write a book and say it is God's word. How can you prove this is not so with your Bible?"* asked Wasyl. *"Because it tells us of the past, present and future which no other book can,"* said thirteen year old Mary. With wry scepticism and a little smugness, Wasyl laid a trap for Mary. *"Then the Bible can tell me when the war is going to end?"* Mary was not perturbed by Wasyl's somewhat facetious question. *"The Bible speaks of the past, present* and future of Jesus Christ, His birth, death, resurrection and ascension, and not about this war," she answered, adding, "but we pray for the defeat of Hitler and the communists."

After a lengthy but goodhearted argument over these questions, Wasyl had had enough. He was tired and cared little for the subject anyway, so he decided to change it to a less challenging one, or so he thought! "Where are you from?" he asked Mary. "You speak Ukrainian but your parents speak Russian." "I am not their daughter," replied Mary. "My parents died about four years ago. My sister was taken in by another Christian family in the next village. We all call each other 'brothers and sisters' because we belong to the family of the Lord."

Once again the subject of Jesus Christ came up. Wasyl tried to steer the conversation away from religion again. "You must miss them terribly," he said, stoking the fire. "Only a little bit," said Mary in a soft voice. "Why? Were they bad parents? I want desperately to be with my parents," said Wasyl. Momentarily pausing from her work, in a quiet voice Mary then told Wasyl she had been brought up as a Christian. The communists had taken her parents and they had suffered terribly at their hands. It was better for them to be with their Lord. After a moment's silence, she staggered Wasyl when she turned to him and said joyfully, "But I will see them again!"

Now Wasyl was really confused, a discussion like this was not what he wanted, but curiosity compelled him to ask for an explanation! "How can you expect to see them again if they are dead?" he exclaimed, perplexity written all over his face. After all, he had seen first-hand the grim finality of death on the battlefield and all around him. In her childlike way, Mary began to explain the towering assurance which Christians have in the death, burial and resurrection of Christ. Because He arose from among the dead, death has no sting, the grave has no victory[20].

This was too much for Wasyl. He asked, "Can I see this book called the Bible?". "I am sorry," she said. "There are only two Bibles in the whole village. When they meet in the *night, the Christians divide into two groups, one Bible for each group. During the day, the Bibles are passed around. You can see one when they return tonight if you wish."* There the conversation with Mary ended.

Along with the others, Wasyl had been allotted a place on the floor to sleep. He stretched out on the bed of straw, drawing his coat over his body. *"Strange people,"* he said to himself as he lay staring at the roof, mulling over his conversation with Mary.

About an hour later, the others returned. Wasyl pretended to be asleep. He felt the cold blast of air as they entered through the front door. *"Our visitor is asleep!"* said one of the men. *"Did he say who he was, where he came from or where he was going?"* he asked Mary. *"He did not mention anything about himself at all,"* she replied. *"But he does want to see the Bible and he asked about the meeting and the Lord Jesus Christ."*

The next morning they asked Wasyl to tell them about himself. At first he was careful not to mention that he was fleeing the Russian army and was a prisoner of war. After a long talk, *Trofim* (the woodcutter) and his wife *Maria* asked if he would like to stay with them as the other five men had done. Well, Wasyl was ecstatic! *"Yes, yes,"* he said without hesitation. At last he had a warm, dry place to sleep and would not have to scrounge for food.

That night after dinner, out of a begging curiosity and in response to their invitation, he accompanied them to the Bible study. They trudged through the snow to the meeting place, guided through the darkness by a lantern. Many others had already assembled within the large single room when Wasyl arrived. Not only was there no fire, there were no seats in the room. The men gathered to one side, the women, their heads kerchiefed in reverential obedience to the word of God[21], stood on the other side. After a few minutes, the silence was broken when one of the men began to read from a book, which Wasyl took to be the Bible. The reading continued for about an hour, after which they sang a number of hymns. There were only a few hymn books, but they all knew the hymns by heart. Wasyl made little sense of the reading but he was able to understand the singing. They sang about Jesus Christ and Him being their Lord and Saviour.

Well, this was not anything like a communist meeting. These people were happy, their faces wore smiles, even without vodka - a significant observation as far as Wasyl was concerned! No one looked or acted like an informer. Their songs of devotion were sung with deep sincerity, orchestrated by joy not fear. They had come together because they wanted to, and not as the result of intimidation.

There were many things about these Christians that puzzled Wasyl, notably, the absence of a priest or even anybody who looked like one. After attending a number of these gatherings, he never saw or heard mention of any human priest that was, is, or will be. Wasyl had always associated churches and religion with priests. Their official regalia and ceremonial rituals were the subject of anti-religious propaganda in the USSR. There was no one here who wore robes, carried a sceptre or donned a mitre! Instead, there appeared to be a number of men - elders, who had responsibility for the corporate spiritual activities of these Christians. Further, all the brethren (the men) had liberty to speak and pray during the course of the meetings. Trofim spoke of secret gatherings under communism, and how some of their company had "disappeared". But now, church services were permitted and priests had resumed their work. So where was the priest who officiated over this church?

Years later, Wasyl came to learn that these Christians had discovered and entered into the blessed truth that all believers are priests. The existence of a presiding class or clergy over the people of God is, in fact, a denial of the gracious legacy of Christ's death, resurrection and ascension. For we know from the Scriptures that all believers are *"...kings and priests unto God and His Father"*[22]. Significantly, it is the apostle Peter who declares to the

Christians, *"ye also, as lively stones, are built up a spiritual house, an holy priesthood, to offer up spiritual sacrifices, acceptable to God by Jesus Christ"* [23] (our Great High Priest). What a glorious and elevating truth this is, and it would be good if more Christians entered into its divine and bountiful provision. We are all priests! With this privilege we have the right and the responsibility to intercede for ourselves and for others before God, to *"offer the sacrifice of praise to God continually, that is, the fruit of our lips..."* [24]. These believers had not only seen this great truth, they were walking according to it, bearing witness to Wasyl, and indeed to the heavenly hosts who are watching, that they are part of an *"holy nation"*, a *"royal priesthood"* [25] whom Christ has called *"out of darkness into His marvellous light"* [26].

There was, too, in the course of these meetings, a simplicity which brought a real sense of the divine presence, without any of the lifeless rituals, grand pomp and ceremonial artifices commonplace among many church gatherings. And, that palpable presence seemed to make all those that gathered there to have a life redolent of Christ! It was not the mortal priest in their midst, for there was none, but *"having an High Priest over the house of God,"* they were able to *"draw near with a true heart in full assurance of faith"* [27]. It was He who promised, *"for where two or three are gathered together in My name, there am I in the midst of them"* [28].

When we gather together as believers, it is to our profit and to His glory that we remember that if there be any spiritual worth in our gathering, it is because of His presence, not ours! Whether it be a dusty Damascus road, the threshing floor of Ornan the Jebusite, or a bare, fireless wooden hut in a forest in the Ukraine, it is the Lord in the midst that is all important. Was it not so on that road to Emmaus? The unmoveable foundation of the entire spiritual edifice of the Church in its universal and local aspects is the presence of the Son of the living God[29]. It we fail to keep this signal truth before us, we will come to deny the all-sufficiency of His presence in collective worship and praise, by the introduction of methods and modes that flatter the flesh but fail the spirit!

And so, those few people meeting in that room in the forest laid hold of this indomitable promise and claimed no lesser value in their coming together, than if their numbers had been many more. Neither did the meagre appointments and crude appearance of that forest shack lessen their communion with their Lord, the Son of Man, who, during His earthly sojourn had nowhere to lay His head. And, if this be the case, we are constrained to ask, why is it that many Christians need towering spires and stained glass windows in ornate buildings within which to worship, things that contain so much of man and so little of God? The power and nobility of the Christian faith is not seen by gazing upon architectural form, awe inspiring though it may be, but by beholding the majesty of the Lion who is the Lamb, who sits in divine regal splendour at the right hand of God[30].

Furthermore, Trofim and these other Christians did not fit into the mould cast by communist propaganda. Their faith appeared to be an intelligent one, not the stuff of suffering fools or pious professors. They had a profound, personal knowledge of what they believed, a reasoned stance and a sober disposition.

When the meeting ended, the Christians mingled in friendly conversation. Wasyl learned that many were refugees from German occupation. He approached a man whose name was Ivan. *"Where are you from and why did you come to this village?"* he asked. Ivan replied in a sombre tone, *"I had to flee my village just before the Germans entered to make reprisals and take male hostages. I left behind my wife, six children and just two loaves of bread for them."* *"This must make you very sad and anxious,"* said Wasyl. *"Yes, I miss them so much, but there is no use in dwelling on it. They are in my heart always and I continually ask my Lord to watch over them. I am sure His hand is on them!"*

Wasyl remembered his conversation with Mary and the confidence she had in her Lord Jesus Christ. These people had something special. This was no sullen repining brotherhood! They seemed to have an enduring hope amidst all the hardship and suffering! With an air of abandonment, Wasyl looked away and said, *"I wish I could have your peace of mind!"* *"You can,"* said Ivan taking hold of Wasyl by the shoulders. *"Put your faith and trust in the Lord Jesus Christ. But you must pray, confess your sin, and believe on Him."* This confused Wasyl. He could understand it if he had to swear an oath of allegiance, or sign a pledge of loyalty before some NKVD official, but to pray to Jesus Christ! This was impossible!

He confessed his difficulty to Ivan who replied, *"Were you too proud to beg food from strangers, or for your very life, or to pray to God to escape German bullets? You had a need. It was beg or starve, a matter of life or death! Now, too, you need to dismiss your pride and pray before the people for your eternal life. You must realise you have a spiritual need."*

Ivan's counsel took root in Wasyl's heart and mind. He had prayed to God and was saved from death when fighting the Germans. He knew he had miraculously been kept alive, often when all around gave way.

Wasyl attended the meetings night after night listening to the gospel of God's grace. With each attendance he became more convicted of his need for salvation, but he procrastinated, failing to take that step of belief. Sadly, many falter at the very threshold of faith. There are instances of man's indecision and consequent eternal loss recorded in the Word of God, to alert us to the folly of neglecting so great a salvation. One such is a Roman governor called Felix. *"And as he* (Paul) *reasoned of righteousness, temperance, and judgement to come, Felix trembled and answered, Go thy way for this time; when I have a convenient season, I will call for thee."* [31] Felix trembled when the apostle brought before him the consequences of his sin and his intemperate life. There is a righteous God who is known by His judgments, One who commands *all* men and women to repent, not willing that *any* should perish[32]. Felix was concerned, even convicted to the point of trembling, but alas, he was never converted! He never confessed his sin and felt his need of the saving grace of God!

Indeed, it may be offensive to us (as it was to Wasyl), to be told that we are sinners in need of God's grace, for we pride ourselves in our virtue. It is not, however, a matter of the absence of virtue in us, for Scripture itself speaks of, for example, an honourable and gracious Samaritan. The annals of man record many deeds of great nobility that cannot and must not be discounted. It is rather a matter of our unrighteousness, that is, our failed standing and natural condition in relation to God's measure of right and wrong. Our unrighteous standing before God springs from Adam's failure. As our federal head, his fallen position has condemned all generations which came through him, for *"...by one man's disobedience many were made sinners..."* [33].

The declaration that we are under God's judgement because of Adam's disobedience and fallen nature, may rail against our notion of natural justice. But, there it is in Holy Writ, emphatic and absolute! By the disobedience of one, the first man, says Paul, many were made sinners. If the reader has a quarrel here, it is not with the writer, but with God and the clear declaration of Scripture![34] Our response to this decree will never affect its truth, because the Word of God is settled in heaven, forever![35] No manner of speculation, argument or weight of opinion for or against, is needed to confirm it, or is able to confound it. But it is not only this proclamation. Each and every holy decree is beyond the reach of man, principalities and powers. So, the believer rests on this unassailable and ineffable truth, hiding within his heart that which is eternally settled in heaven, that, *"by the obedience of One, shall many be made righteous"* [36].

Can the purest amongst us in all honesty claim exemption from the charge within Holy Writ that *"..all have sinned, and come short of the glory of God"*? [37] We can come to Him only as sinners in need of His pardon. We can come only through His Son, the singular solitary exception to this indictment! Try to meet God on the basis of intellect and we soon find, as did Saul of Tarsus, that His foolishness is greater than our wisdom[38]. Try to be reconciled to God through our good works and we are duly informed that all our personal righteousnesses are as "filthy rags" before Him[39], that it is by grace we are saved through faith and not through our works, lest any should boast[40]. We may try to seek Him through our exalted status among men, but find as did Naaman long ago, that God is no respecter of persons. If we approach Him on the basis of our attempt to keep His moral laws, we, with the self-righteous Pharisees and bewitched Galatians, earn nothing save rebuke, *"for through the deeds of the law shall no flesh be justified"* in the sight of God[41]. In law, God demanded righteousness from us. In grace He has provided it for us through His Son. If we accept through faith, His death as propitiation for us, we become the righteousness of God in Him![42] Should we seek to gain His pardon at the final great judgement through a plea of "honest doubt", we will be justly condemned, as we are without excuse, for the heavens declare the glory of God and the firmament shows His handiwork[43].

There are ways that seem right unto us, but the ends thereof are the ways of death! There is but one way to life eternal, the path we take by faith to the cross of Christ, as sinners, wholly relying upon His grace. Christ said, *"I am the way, the truth, and the life: no man cometh unto the Father, but by Me"* [44]. Are we prepared to cry as did the publican, *"God be merciful to me a sinner,"* and the prodigal son, *"Father, I have sinned against heaven and before Thee,"* [45] or, are we like the Pharisee who exalted himself saying, *"God, I thank Thee, that I am not as other men are, extortioners, unjust, adulterers,.."*[46]? Until we utter the cry of the publican or the prodigal, until the truth of sin in standing and sin in life be known in our inward parts, let there be no mistake, according to Scripture we will never come to know God or be reconciled to Him who is the God of Abraham, Isaac and Jacob; the God who spoke and the worlds came into being; the God whose only begotten Son declared *"I am not come to call the righteous, but sinners to repentance."* [47]

And, what is repentance? It is the abiding, universal necessity of discovering and accepting our abject unrighteousness and condemnation before God; and then, our turning to trust Him for salvation!

Be assured, there is a heaven to be gained and an everlasting punishment to be avoided![48] Eternal punishment! There can be no more solemn prospect facing the unbeliever, a prospect not dismissed by agnostic thought[49]. Let the words of Christ be the final evangel here; the One who, because of His love to mankind, spoke more of the impending eternal punishment awaiting the unbeliever, than of the heaven awaiting the believer: *"For God so loved the world, that He gave His only begotten Son, that whosoever believeth in Him should not perish, but have everlasting life"*[50].

> *Out of Christ, without a Saviour,*
> *Give to Him now your heart,*
> *Ere the door of mercy closes,*
> *And you hear His word, "Depart."*
> Davis & Beveridge

Wasyl's conversion

During the Bible study one night, Wasyl was particularly troubled about what he had heard concerning his state before God. He had often come close to death. What if he should die without being reconciled to God? He was now sure God existed. Vodka offered no lasting solace and communism could offer no hope.

He knew it was not enough to believe that God existed; he had to seek redemption and pardon from Him. He understood the only way was to confess his sinful position before God and receive His Son as his personal Redeemer. One night, having once again sat in the meeting and listened to the message of man's ruin and God's remedy, in prayer he accepted Christ as his Lord and Saviour. This was the second time he had seriously turned to God in prayer. On that first occasion, he sought salvation from German bullets and bayonets. Now, he was seeking his soul's salvation!

There was great rejoicing among the Christians and that little room, though fireless and shrouded by snow, exuded a warmth and a glow that Wasyl never forgot. He was now a Christian, and knowingly at peace with God, a peace based on the imperishable foundation, that Christ *"..was delivered for our offences, and raised again for our justification"* [51]. This peace was not the product of looking for an inward feeling or mystic revelation. Peace with God came only when his soul rested on the assurance given by the Word of God. "It is written" is ever the divine ground of faith and peace. Being justified by his faith, he now had peace with God[52].

The men embraced and kissed him in their customary manner. Wasyl thought he had to kiss the women also so he turned to an old lady next to him and proceeded to give her a kiss. She was quite surprised at his overture, as this was not part of their custom. *"Just kiss the men, brother, not the women!"* Wasyl's misapprehension brought a round of well meaning laughter from them all!

Before leaving, an old man drew alongside Wasyl and said, *"Praise the Lord, you are now saved and belong to Him. Now the real evidence of this will be when you are baptised in water."* Wasyl had yet to learn the significance of water baptism.

Two months had now passed since that first encounter with Trofim in the forest. Wasyl had been fortified physically and spiritually. He spent his days doing odd jobs for his hosts and the Christians in the village. In the evenings, he never failed to attend the Bible studies, for now they were times of great joy and encouragement. His fervent desire to know more about the Bible and about Christ led him to copy by hand the entire gospel of John. It was within this holy and inspired book that he came to know more of the deity of Christ, His eternal Sonship and co-equality with God the

Father. But more! In the glad tidings of this fourth Gospel, Wasyl saw the anchor that secured the faith of his little orphaned friend Mary, and of Ivan, the father of six children. *"Let not your heart be troubled: ye believe in God, believe also in Me. In My Father's house are many mansions: if it were not so, I would have told you. I go to prepare a place for you. And if I go and prepare a place for you, I will come again, and receive you unto Myself; that where I am, there ye may be also."* [53]

Time to leave again

At times, Wasyl's preoccupation with his new found faith and friends allowed him to forget he was wanted by the Red Army and was an escaped prisoner of war. Through his good friend, the village administrator, Trofim managed to obtain refugee registration papers for Wasyl. For the most part, the Germans left refugees alone. Recently, however, the Germans had become panicky and suspicious because of significant losses to the allies. Furthermore, the Russians were advancing and were not far away. This small village of Novomyrovka could become a trap for a Red soldier fleeing the Red Army. Trofim suggested that Wasyl should leave and make his way to somewhere safer.

So early one cold, bleak morning, he reluctantly stepped out of the cottage that had been for him a place of refuge and comfort. It was a very sad moment. Farewells had been said the previous night. He was leaving behind cherished times with the Christians, the Bible studies and the convivial chats around the fire after dinner. He began to experience again the familiar pangs of despair as he contemplated once again becoming an itinerant beggar, having to hide from the Germans and outrun the Russians.

However, the overwhelming despondency lifted as he began to count his blessings. Maria, Trofim, little Mary, Ivan and the other Christians had assured him of their continual prayers for his wellbeing and safety. He had a store of food, warm clothes and identity papers secured by Trofim's friend and, of course, in his pocket, his hand-written copy of the fourth Gospel. Above all, he knew this time he was not going to be travelling alone. The Good Shepherd of John's gospel was with him[54]. Wasyl now had a friend that would never leave him nor forsake him [55].

It was his new identity as a child of God that was all important now! He had a family according to the ties of nature, but he was now also in God's spiritual family through faith in the person of His only begotten Son.

There is a notion at large that all people are God's children. It is a quaint doctrine, founded on sentiment rather than Scripture, and often quoted by misguided religious leaders to galvanise popularity amongst the people, cajole their laity, or humour politicians. Let the words of Christ again be the final arbiter on this matter: *"But as many as received Him, to them gave He power* (authority) *to become the children of God, even to them that believe on His name."* [56] Those who have not so received and believed, remain in the family of the fallen first man, Adam. His penalty rests on them. Only those who have believed and trusted Christ are in God's family, with His Son Jesus Christ, the second Man and last Adam, as its Risen Head[57]. As believers, they rest on His victory. What a blessed truth this is! This is what is meant by the Lord's instruction to Nicodemus *"..ye must be born again"*[58]. Wasyl, and all who believe in Christ as Saviour and Lord, are born into a new family, the spiritual family of God.

Joining the evacuees

Wasyl continued his sojourn westwards and by the end of January 1944 he had entered Moldavia, a German occupied Soviet republic known for its agriculture, particularly grapes and wine. There were no lush vineyards or furrowed fields now, only a blanket of deep late January snow over the land. As he emerged from the cover of some trees, he saw lines of people moving in dogged silence along the snow-bound road. As far as he could make out through the falling snow, there were no soldiers with them. He saw old men and women dragging their meagre belongings in makeshift sleds, young women with children, and mothers carrying infants, all heading westward. Who were these people and where were they from?

He approached them and discreetly merged into their ranks. No one took any notice. After a few hundred metres, Wasyl asked the man next to him, *"Who are all these people and where have you come from?"* *"We are evacuees from German occupied regions,"* came the reply, the man not bothering to turn his head. *"How is it that the Germans allow you to walk freely?"* asked Wasyl.

The man replied, *"Many of us are people who were persecuted by the communists for our political and religious beliefs. When the Red Army began to purge their opponents, we fled and were caught by the Germans. They knew we hated communism and they gave us registration papers which allow us to travel west and also obtain food. We have no love for facism, but we hate communism more. These papers are our chance to travel west and try to get to Canada or England."* (There was another boy, Mickey, from Kharkov who, unknown to Wasyl, was travelling this way with his family, with whom he was to meet after the war and form a lasting friendship.)

Wasyl decided to tag along with these people as there was safety in numbers and the real prospect of getting a regular food supply. Some had already shared their scant provisions with him.

After several kilometres, just before nightfall, they stopped and made camp. This meant finding a sheltered place to sleep, usually a dug-out under scrub or in a makeshift shelter from branches. Suddenly his preparations came to a halt. There, as bold as life itself, was a face he recognised. *"Simon!"* he whispered in disbelief! Then as their gaze met, he declared, *"Simon, Simon it is you!"* It was indeed! Simon was one of the Christians, a tailor in the village of Novomyrovka. He had managed to obtain proper papers from the Germans, entitling him to food rations, and giving him a chance to travel west. *"You must walk with me. I have good papers and I will share all my food rations with you,"* said Simon.

So Wasyl and Simon teamed together, sharing whatever they had. During the cold nights they took turns to wear their only coat between them. One would sleep using the coat as a blanket while the other walked around to keep warm. There were two older "Christian" men travelling with the refugees, who never really endeared themselves to Wasyl or Simon. They learned later that they were communist spies.

Wasyl   Simon

ID photographs when evacuees in Germany, 1944-45

CHAPTER 6

Liberation: Journeying On

After several weeks of trekking through snow-bound eastern Europe, they had crossed Moldavia and Romania, and entered Hungry. Here the local officials were not so accommodating. Although under German occupation and despite having an agreement with Germany, these officials were willing to supply only water to the evacuees. However, the Hungarian people themselves found it in their hearts to give them whatever spare food they had. Wasyl remembered how the villagers graciously responded to the "hand-to-mouth" sign used by his companions. The villagers hid food under their coats and, when walking past, either dropped it within sight or pushed it into the hands of the evacuees.

An SS mentor

It was when this itinerant troop of evacuees reached the Carpathian mountains, that events altered significantly for Wasyl. This nine hundred kilometre chain of rugged mountains arcing from Bratislava in Czechoslovakia and into Romania was going to be difficult to cross. But nature's barrier was not their immediate cause of anxiety. There, in the distance, a German mobile contingent approached at great speed. The vehicles came to a screeching stop. Soldiers jumped out of the trucks and, at gunpoint, began shouting at them to form lines, after which they were marched into a field and told to camp there until further notice. They were given meagre food rations and warned not to have any contact with the

Hungarian people. This quite inexplicable action caused panic, and people began asking, *"What is going on? Why have they suddenly taken us prisoner? What are they going to do with us? Are we going to be shot?"* Wasyl had learned long before this that the Germans became interested in you only if you were a threat, or useful to them.

A week passed and their fate was still unknown. Mass executions of refugees and POWs were common knowledge, but they had German papers and surely the Germans would not shoot them in such an exposed place? Wasyl and Simon committed each day to the Lord. The German guards dispassionately distributed paltry food rations and maintained their grim silence. Each passing day brought increasing anxiety. Some became hysterical. Scant shelter from the bitter cold caused great hardship for the aged, the children and infants. How much longer was this situation to continue? One thing was certain, many would die if they were not given proper shelter and adequate food.

About two weeks later, a small convoy of trucks drove into their camp. Wasyl, Simon and the others were summarily loaded on board and taken to a local railway station where they were herded into cattle trucks. Still no one told them where they were going or why they had been rounded up. As the train pulled away from the town, fear again gripped the people. They were heading north, toward Poland.

The journey was very uncomfortable. Apart from the rank odour of cattle dung, they had to sit on bare floor boards, their bodies jarring with the slightest jolt and sway of the railway truck. At a station stop in Czechoslovakia, the train was surrounded by a menacing band of bearded and bedraggled Czech soldiers, who invited them to join the fight against the Red Army. No one accepted!

After travelling through Poland for some time, the train approached a large town called *Peremyshell*, quite close to the Ukrainian border. Several shrill whistles announced its arrival at the station. The train came to a squealing stop, hissing plumes of steam. There was a flurry of action and the sound of boots stomping in various directions as German guards surrounded the trucks. The doors were opened to check on the evacuees. An officer arrived and shouted, *"No one is to get off the train. You will be shot if you try and escape!"*

Several minutes later, a voice outside the carriage said earnestly in Ukrainian, *"If you don't want to go to Germany, jump out now and run across the tracks to the trees. Those without German papers are going to a POW camp inside Germany!"*

It was time to make a quick decision, as Wasyl had only identity papers issued by the village of Novomyrovka. Instinct told Wasyl and about nine others to jump. There had been alarming reports of the treatment of POWs in German prison camps. To be on the run was safer than to be imprisoned at the mercy of the Germans or be caught by the Red Army once it advanced. Simon decided to go also, even though he did have proper papers. Peering through cracks in the side of the cattle truck, they watched the patrolling guards and calculated on just two minutes between circuits in which to make their dash. The moment came and they were off! They ran over the dirty coal-covered ground and railway tracks, between stationary carriages and mounds of coal, hoping there were no patrols on the perimeter of the rail yard. To be seen would mean certain death!

When they arrived at the trees, breathless and hearts pounding, they were met by the man who had warned them of their fate. He led them to a small room near the railyards. *"You are lucky,"* he said. *"Did you know that they are separating you? Don't be afraid, I have work for you and a safe place to stay."* Wasyl and the others looked at each other with relief and amazement. To be able to work and not have to sleep on the run was almost utopian. Work meant food and shelter! *"Yes, yes, that would be wonderful,"* they said with expectant optimism.

Then came the shock! With consummate indifference, the man said, *"You will be going to work for a German SS officer!"* They stood staring at each other in silent disbelief! Was this some sort of joke? If not, then what trap had they fallen into? Everyone knew of the SS. They were Hitler's counterpart to Stalin's NKVD, charged with annihilation of the enemies of the Third Reich. Many of the terrible excesses they indulged in against the 'enemy' (whoever that was deemed to be) were due to the absolute immunity given to them by the Fuhrer.

The man saw the distraught looks on their faces. *"Don't worry! Don't worry! There is no reason to be afraid. As long as you behave yourselves and work hard, the SS officer will be very nice to you. Believe me, I too work for him! There are others like you who already work for him."*

He then explained the situation. This SS officer was one of two who had been in charge of a "nuts and bolts" factory in Kharkov "vacated" by the local owners when the Germans occupied the Ukraine. When the Red Army began to advance, these two officers, using "volunteers", loaded the factory equipment onto trains and brought it to Peremyshell where they resumed production. This had a threefold benefit; it kept the German command happy by supplying essential materials, they were able to make some profit for themselves and, most importantly, it kept them away from the Russian front.

Where did the evacuees fit into this? POWs from the local prison could not be used for the factory work, so the Ukranian and his fellow SS "business partner" recruited workers from the evacuees passing through Peremyshell railway station!

Wasyl and the others were not exactly reassured by this explanation. After all, their lives were to be dependent upon what appeared to be two SS officers working on the "fiddle"! For the present, they had no choice but to stay in that room overnight. In the morning they were to meet the SS officer himself.

At dawn the Ukrainian escorted them to the factory. Having spent a relatively comfortable night, and with food in their bellies, any immediate concerns were dispelled. They soon arrived at the factory and there, behind the large gates, stood a man in plain clothes. Although the insignia of the SS, the dreaded black uniform adorned with its death heads, was missing, they knew this was the SS officer of whom they had heard. His arrogant stance, hands on hips and legs astride, the luger strapped to his waist, his polished leather boots and mastiff by his side, betrayed his office. Here standing before them was one of Hitler's elite, a "Teutonic Knight" who, according to the code of membership, could trace his Aryan descent to the year 1750.

"Line up and pay attention," shouted the Ukrainian. The SS officer stepped forward with an arrogant swagger and began to address Wasyl and his companions in a non-aggressive but condescending manner. *"I know who you are and I don't care! You can work for me here and I will provide you with food and a room. You will also get an ID card just in case you are questioned by other German officials. I will protect you. But, if you make trouble for me, then I will make big trouble for you!"*

There were a few moments of silence during which they were expected to make up their minds whether or not to stay. In reality, they had little choice, and the German knew it! There was no answer from anyone. The SS officer rightly interpreted their silence to be acceptance of his offer. *"Good,"* he said slapping his whip on his boots. *"Follow this man* (the Ukrainian) *and he will show you where to go and what to do!"*

The SS officer was true to his word. Their arduous schedule required them to work from dawn to dusk six days each week and a half-day on Saturday mornings.

For this they were fed a daily ration of black bread, potato soup and fat, issued with new ID papers and given a room to share. In their "free time" on Sunday afternoons, they would wander through the nearby villages trying to scrounge extra food. There was an element of risk in this despite their new ID papers, not from the German soldiers but from some of the civilians who took exception to those who worked for the enemy. Many of the local people themselves had been forced into labour gangs by the Germans, mainly supplying them with farm produce.

It was now September, 1944. Wasyl and the others who had escaped from the train fell into a pleasant routine, reflecting their improved situation. Besides Simon, there were two other Christians in the group with him. They would often pray, read from Wasyl's hand-written gospel of John and discuss the Scriptures, spending their Sunday afternoons walking through the town and into the country, enjoying their relative liberty.

One morning after rollcall, they were called to meet the SS officer again. This was a rare occasion, as he left all daily supervision to overseers chosen from the evacuees. Their first reaction was that someone was in trouble! He met them, wearing the full regalia of his office, beside him was his ever present hound. He spoke briefly and to the point. *"The Red Army is not far away. Very soon we expect them to be on our doorstep. I am leaving for the Fatherland. As for you, you can stay here or come with me to Germany. It is your decision. Once we are there, you can continue to work for me under the same conditions!"*

He knew very well that these men would not want to stay around to greet the Russians, so it was no surprise when they decided to go with him. After loading all the machinery onto a train, they left Peremyshell for Germany. Two weeks later, the factory was up and running in the town of *Opal*. Wasyl and the other men stayed in disused army barracks just out of the town. There were about five hundred workers in the factory, many conscripted from the town itself.

The Move to Berlin - Hitler's stronghold

The SS officer by now had a thriving business (his partner had left). Once again, however, the Russian advance necessitated a relocation of the factory. The SS officer and his band of workers again loaded the equipment onto a train and sought to re-establish operations in Bamberg. To reach Bamberg the train had to pass through Berlin. Having to enter the citadel of Hitler caused considerable anxiety among the workers. Anticipating their apprehension, their SS mentor assured them all would be well as long as they stayed on the train and kept a low profile.

After a long, bone-shattering journey through Poland and Czechoslovakia, and passing through many towns that had been reduced to rubble by Hitler's blitzkrieg, the train pulled into Berlin station. There was indeed cause for anxiety. The railyards were attended by large numbers of uniformed soldiers and plain clothes men who, no doubt, were the dreaded Gestapo. Trains were coming and going, with several waiting to leave. There was a continual hissing as engines exhaled, the steam moistening the thick acrid air. Blasts of smoke and the sound of grinding metal signalled the departure of trains as they lurched into motion. Frequent shrill whistles from the guards kept Wasyl and the others alert and anxious. There were troop trains and trains loaded with military equipment and supplies. This was a very dangerous place for a Red Army escapee to be! It would be a time of unremitting fear for all of them.

The workers' anxiety increased when they were informed that it would be at least three days before they could leave for Bamberg. The first two harrowing days were spent on the train, just waiting. Their only contact was the SS officer and those who brought them food under his oversight. To allay their anxiety and mitigate the bitter cold, some of those on the train began to ridicule Wasyl, Simon and the other Christians, for they had seen them pray and discuss the Scriptures.

One night their restless slumber was disturbed by distant humming which grew louder. Then the deafening wail of sirens alerted them that planes were overhead. Bombs began to fall relentlessly and exploded in such numbers that it was at times impossible to hear or think! Wasyl and the other Christians huddled in a corner of the carriage. They were joined by the others who grabbed hold of them and cried, *"We are all going to be killed. Please pray to God for us. We are trapped here together. God will protect you and us also if we are close to you. Please stay close to us!"* Wasyl and the believers prayed. After a time, the bombing ceased. The men sat in silence, emotionally exhausted. And there were no more taunts about religion!

The clear, still light of dawn revealed the extent of the devastation. It was not as extensive here as in other parts of Berlin but, alas, sufficient to further delay their departure to Bamberg! The SS officer and others from the German hierarchy came on the scene to inspect the damage and organise reclamation. Troops, civilians and POWs were all mustered to clean up the rubble. Then, around midday, during the clean-up, all eyes lifted from their labours to look into the western sky. Waves of bombers blacked out the sun as they relentlessly flew towards Berlin. Once again bombs in their thousands rained on the city and its environs. These were the Americans on their daylight bombing raids over Germany.

As the Germans ran for cover, many of them would have remembered Hitler's arrogant boast that Berlin would never become a target for Allied bombs! Wasyl and his companions hid under the train, enduring explosion after explosion. Breathing was difficult due to the pungent gasses released by burning fuel and materials in the railyard. After the dust had cleared and the skies were again empty, Germans, POWs, evacuees and civilians emerged from their places of refuge in stunned silence. Many did not!

Reclamation began once again, but not without incident. During a methodical audit of damage, the Germans discovered that a box of cheese had been stolen from a supply train. At first, enquiries correctly laid the blame on POWs from one of the trains. They were to be shot as saboteurs. However, they pleaded their innocence and blamed the theft on the evacuees who, of course, were Russians. This seemed plausible to the Gestapo investigators. To them it was also desirable that Russians should be found culpable. Moreover, someone had to be seen to pay, not so much for the missing box of cheese, but for the audacity of Allied bombing of Germany's premier city.

The Gestapo demanded the SS officer release the alleged perpetrators. They wanted three scapegoats. He protested vehemently, *"If my men have done this, then I will punish them!"* *"Good,"* they said, *"We will wait here and see that you do!"* The SS officer had no option and grabbed three from the group. Wasyl was one of them! They were paraded before the others, soundly berated and then tied firmly onto the railway carriage. *"See,"* he said to the Gestapo, *"Now when the train moves, they will be dragged along!"* They departed, smiling vindictively.

What would happen now? Apart from the terrifying prospect of being dragged to death, there was really nothing, save the grace of God, to prevent the Gestapo from returning and shooting them. But something else heightened their fear. There, in the distant sky, the "eagles" appeared once again. In minutes they were over the city and the railyards, unleashing their deadly "apples" as they were called. Wasyl and the two with him were caught, helpless, in the open. Bombs exploded all around them.

Their wrists burned and cut as they strained on the ropes that bound them to the carriage. It was a time for earnest prayer again!

After the raid, the other evacuees, the SS officer and the Gestapo rushed out expecting to find them dead. *"You see what happens to you when you make trouble,"* said the SS man sternly, shaking his finger in their faces. Wasyl, who was hanging by his wrists "legless", could hardly hear far less comprehend what the officer was saying, as the bombing had left him stunned and disoriented. The Germans went about their business, leaving them tied to the train.

Later, when he was sure the Gestapo had gone, their SS mentor approached and said, *"I am sorry, I had to do this to you, otherwise you would have been shot."* He released them saying, *"Go and stay out of sight in the carriage. The Gestapo have more important things to do now."* With aching and bleeding limbs, they quickly scrambled into the carriage. Wasyl had been saved from death yet again! *"God must really be with you,"* the others said. *"Even the two with you who are not Christians were prayed for and have been saved."* The Christians rejoiced that, through this, they were able to bear witness to the grace of God.

The next day, the SS officer arrived with good news. They were to leave for Bamberg in a few hours.

The end of the war in Europe - May, 1945

Bamberg was a large town, situated north of München and east of Frankfurt. Nurnberg was about sixty kilometres to the south. The factory was soon established again and in full production.

Early one May morning, the SS officer addressed the workers. *"The Americans will soon be upon the town. I have been sent to the front. I suggest you don't stay here. It will be better for you in the forest. Wait there for the Americans. Make sure you go to the forest west of the town. There will be fighting in the forest to the east. Be careful, the Gestapo are executing suspicious people on the spot."* He turned on his heels and left, never to be seen by them again. Some weeks later, Wasyl learned of his death in a battle not very far from Bamberg. He had mixed feelings about this man. On the one hand he represented the terrible infamy of the Third Reich, on the other, he had displayed a definite kindness to them.

At any rate, the message was clear and no time was lost fleeing to the forest. The SS officer had left some food for them during their escape. Wasyl and his friends spent three days hiding in relative safety, even though the confrontation between the advancing Americans and retreating Germans took place south, instead of east, of the town.

New Masters - Arrival of the Americans!

Bamberg was soon occupied by the American army. This was a dangerous time, as lawlessness prevailed until the Americans established a system of order. Many of the displaced people and evacuees looted the stores and vacant houses. Assaults were common, especially on German soldiers found hiding or trying to escape.

After about a week, the Americans installed a form of civil order using local citizens as "police". They were issued with weapons but were not permitted to use them unless their lives were threatened. All infractions of the peace were to be reported to the American authorities.

Despite the initial unrest, Wasyl was overjoyed at the presence of the Allies. The evacuees had felt a tremendous relief when they saw a column of American footsoldiers marching towards the town. Strange accents and smiles met them. The few remaining Germans, too, were relieved that the Americans reached Bamberg before the Russians. Stalin was not a signatory to the Geneva Convention, resulting in terrible brutality occurring between the now victorious Red Army and the Germans.

The passing weeks saw more Americans arrive in Bamberg. Out of sympathy and necessity, their attention turned to the evacuees, many more of whom had fled to Bamberg, among them displaced Soviet soldiers and POWs. The Yalta conference in the Crimea between Churchill, Rooseveldt and Stalin, agreed that displaced people should be repatriated to their home land. To this end, the Americans were required to round up and confine all displaced persons in detention camps, pending repatriation.

The Americans, however, were unprepared for the stiff resistance they found among the evacuees, many preferring suicide to going home. Wasyl saw people jump from buildings, or throw themselves into the river, one case involving a mother and her children.

The bewildered Americans called a meeting of the evacuees. *"The war is over and you should go home. Why don't you want to go home? Why commit suicide?"* They told them, *"If we go home, we will either be killed or be sent to a prison camp in Siberia!"* The Americans were not unsympathetic, just unbelieving, asking the Soviets to "reassure" the evacuees. The NKVD obliged, but they were too afraid to address the evacuees alone. Even when accompanied by the Americans, they received a very hostile reception. Initially, the Americans refused to repatriate anyone against their will, stating it was "undemocratic" to do so. However, the NKVD insisted that the conditions of the Yalta conference be adhered to. So the repatriations continued and so did the suicides. Some evacuees had crossed the border and had seen how their fellows were mistreated. Others, through misplaced faith, believed that because they were captured while fighting the enemy and the war had ended victoriously, they would not be punished. They were proved so wrong!

By doing odd jobs, Wasyl and his companions were able to hire a room in a nearby village, thereby avoiding being placed in a detention camp and repatriated to Russia. After a few weeks they moved on, travelling from village to village, keeping close to the forests.

Wasyl was always on the look-out for Christians. He not only desired their fellowship, but he wanted to obtain a Bible. In one particular town he was told of some Christians that met in a house. He wondered if these meetings would be like those with Trofim and the others in Novomyrovka. One evening he presented himself to them and found them very gracious and welcoming. Two ladies, aged in their fifties, conducted the meetings, gathering with two other women and their children. Their husbands were missing. Wasyl visited them often and enjoyed their fellowship.

One day he met a young lad who informed him of a Baptist church not far away. The lad remembered it because of the number of young girls attending the meetings. Now this was very encouraging to Wasyl in at least two respects. He had found another Christian gathering and he had come to know about some young women of like faith.

He told the two Christian ladies about the Baptist church and his intended visit. They, and one of Wasyl's companions, a Ukrainian man called *Deribas,* went with him. They had to walk about ten kilometres to get to the church. The gospel of God's grace was preached and Deribas was saved. This was a remarkable event for Wasyl because Deribas often chided him over his faith in Christ. Afterwards, he told Wasyl that he deliberately provoked him to test his Christian virtue. Wasyl had learned two lessons, first *"the Lord's hand is not shortened, that it cannot save; neither is His ear heavy, that it cannot hear"*[59]. Second, how import is patience and turning the other cheek!

Baptism

Wasyl heard of a group of Christians in München. His

yearning desire was to own a Bible and they may have a spare one, he thought! However, he had been thinking about baptism because the two Christian ladies had stated it was essential for salvation. He was confused and concerned over this but knew little of the scriptural teaching regarding this doctrine. All he knew was that the Lord wanted him to be baptised. His understanding could wait, his obedience could not! After contacting the Christians at München, he discovered some of them also desired baptism. It was decided that Wasyl would travel to München and join their baptismal service. On the 3rd of March, 1946, Wasyl, Deribas and about thirty-six other believers were baptised in an indoor swimming pool in München.

Later, Wasyl would learn more fully the truth concerning New Testament baptism. Christianity is faith in a Person, not a religion. It is not by undergoing certain rituals (eg infant sprinkling), that a person becomes a Christian; we will not find such practices enjoined in God's Word. Neither does a person become a Christian by coveting and living the kind of life that Christians are exhorted to lead. As the believers in Novomyrovka had declared, Wasyl was saved and became a Christian the moment he placed his faith in Christ as Saviour and Lord. Baptism, immersion in water, is a public expression of that faith, an outward witness and identification with the death, burial and resurrection of Christ[60]. It is wholly a step of obedience, a profession *of* salvation, never a step *to* it. Perhaps the reader is one who has trusted Christ as Saviour, but is not baptised! If you believe, what hinders you? We, as believers, are challenged by the words of Christ, as was Wasyl, *"Why call ye me, 'Lord, Lord', and do not the things which I say?"* [61]

A Bible

It was in a town called *Erlangen* that Wasyl received a Bible, in a parcel postmarked America. It was his very own, given to him by a person or persons unknown. It was the most precious gift anyone could have given him. The joy and deep appreciation he experienced was so great, that it sparked and fuelled a passionate life-long commitment to bring similar happiness to others who had no access to the Word of God. God had spared his life many times and in return he would devote his life to telling others about His Saviour.

He would often visit München, walking among the bombed buildings, Bible in hand. The civil authorities had already done much to clear the ruins, but the streets were still dangerous because of collapsing walls. Even the vibrations of a passing tram could precipitate a fall of tonnes of rubble but, no matter, he was now in possession of the complete inspired Word of God.

Christian camp: Swartzenberg, Germany - 1946

Musical interlude

Town life was becoming more orderly and there was more time for the people to pursue peace-time activities. The Baptist church had organised a training camp for young Christians near *Swartzenberg*. Wasyl attended the camp and soon developed his natural talent for music. There was a piano available and he practised fervently each day until he was able to sight read the music of more straightforward tunes. Later, he acquired an old mandolin which he used to hone his musical skills.

Wasyl stayed with the Christians and often visited the two Christian ladies and the Baptist church. They assisted him and his friends with food and shelter when needed. Although not permitted to sell food, many of the farmers gave willingly to the displaced persons when asked. Some even agreed to allow displaced people to "steal" their livestock, reporting the loss as a theft to cover themselves with the officials. Wasyl recounted with great mirth how a group of displaced persons "kidnapped" a cow from a field without leaving a trace. They put old boots over the cow's hooves so as not to leave prints in the snow. They even hid the cow on the third storey of an old farm house, having coaxed it up the three flights of stairs! The authorities were nonplussed as to the location of the stolen cow, even though they knew who the thieves were. In the end they gave up, simply requesting that the perpetrators explain the mysterious disappearance. This they did to the great amusement of all!

Wasyl and his companions now had time to laugh a little and reflect philosophically on life around them. Communist propaganda continually insisted that the working classes in the West were impoverished. Here they were in the midst of capitalism. They had entered the homes of labourers and factory workers and had seen their superior welfare. Their homes had electricity, running water, proper beds and even separate rooms for eating, sleeping and living! There were toilet rooms and septic tanks, much to the amazement of Russian soldiers, who thought toilet bowls were hand basins. The usual deprivations of war existed, of course, but an exploited working class? Not here! Where was the accelerating economic exploitation that would impoverish the people, provoking them to overthrow the onerous capitalist oligarchy? "Is not this Germany, the birth place of Marx, the progenitor of communism and, according to his predictions and the propaganda, the mainspring of communism in Europe?"

These questions were asked by many Soviet soldiers as they marched from behind the Iron Curtain of communist propaganda into western Europe. They had been kept in ignorance and been lied to by the 'Party', and many defected as their disbelief turned to disillusionment and then to despair and disgust!

After some time, Wasyl and his companions returned to Bamberg. There they were able to earn a little money doing odd-jobs for the civic authority. Wasyl's job was to help clear the waterways of debris. The bombing had clogged the rivers, making them hazardous for transport. It was dangerous work! Unexploded bombs lay buried in the sludge necessitating the use of men to dive for the debris beneath the water. There were fatalities and injuries. Wasyl's arm still bears the scar from a deep gash caused by diving too close to the metal remains of a bridge.

One day the town was again troubled by NKVD officials seeking displaced Soviet citizens for repatriation. This time, however, the Americans sided with the displaced people. Any displaced person seeking political asylum would not be repatriated. In fact, the Americans encouraged them to change their names and adopt new identities. The terrible fate of those previously repatriated had now come to light, causing this change in official policy not only from the Americans, but also from the British. Both countries now thoroughly distrusted the Soviet Communist government, laying the foundation of the Cold War which would develop for many decades to come.

Displaced Persons' camp, destiny England, 1948

Under these liberal conditions, Wasyl and his companions decided to rejoin the displaced persons' camp. Here they were given food and clothing and would be listed for emmigration to the USA, Canada, or Britain. Wasyl wanted to go to Canada. However, the officials, displaced people themselves, took exception to Wasyl nominating himself as a Christian, and denied him a choice of destination. When his turn came for listing, the official stated bluntly, *"You have been selected to go to Britain, but you can choose to work on a farm, in a factory or in a mine."* Wasyl had to give this some thought. Factory work did not appeal to him. Working on a farm would not be expedient. His overriding desire was to go to Canada and, if he chose farm work, they might send him to some isolated region, making his prospects of getting to Canada too difficult. Consequently, he chose the mines. He was not told what sort of mines they were, just that they were in Danby in the north of England. Deribas left earlier, having been sent to work on a farm. Simon decided to stay in Germany.

Wasyl (top left), Simon (top middle) and Deribas (bottom right) - Germany 1946, prior to Wasyl leaving for the UK

A few days later he received his papers and travel documents. He was now, for the purposes of travel, classified as a displaced Polish national on route to the mines in England. A train took him, and many other displaced persons, from Bamberg to a holding camp in *Munster*, quite some distance northwest of Nurnberg. From Munster they were taken to Holland, where a steamer would transport them to England. Even though there were few stops, the journey took quite some time, giving Wasyl a chance to see more of the superior living conditions of the West. It appeared as if the whole population of western Europe was in transit. Intermittent lines of people criss-crossed the landscape, moving to all points of the compass, some in trains, others in assorted vehicles, and many walking with their meagre belongings on their backs or in makeshift carts. The displaced of Europe were still making their way home. In Wasyl's case, it was a case of finding one! It was an important matter which he had earnestly placed before his Lord. As they crossed the border into Holland he was quite taken with the windmills and water systems. Good progress had been made in repairing war damage and many towns had regained their lighting.

The journey ended at the waterfront somewhere in Holland. They spent a claustrophobic night on the train and after breakfast they were to board a steamer. The docks had come alive with the sound of men shouting, steam whistles, the clanging of cranes and the strange, melancholy cries of the gulls. Indeed, the whole dockside was a source of wonder to him. There were different types of vessels, merchant ships as well as gunboats, huge cranes that lifted merchandise into and out of the ships. What amazed him most was the huge expanse of ocean known as the North Sea leading to the English Channel. He had seen lakes before, and even crossed a large stretch of water in the Ukraine, but this was something else! The air too had a distinctive smell, salty, cold and bracing.

Before long, Wasyl, and about five hundred other refugees, Serbs, Russians, Poles, Hungarians, Ukrainians and other Europeans, boarded a steamer and were sent down into a large hold. Wasyl had never seen, let alone travelled on, such a vessel as this, and marvelled at how such a large amount of iron could float. An hour or so later, he felt vibrations as the engines started, followed by movement as the steamer pulled away from the wharf. A few blasts of the steam whistle confirmed that they were on their way to England.

The channel crossing was typically rough and the stuffy conditions in the hold exacerbated Wasyl's queasiness. After a time he became used to the roll of the ship and began thinking about the past. His mind flitted between thoughts of home, his family and his future. He had often wondered about his brothers, had they survived the war and if so, where were they? Were his mother and father still alive? His sisters, what had become of them? He yearned to see them all and tell of his conversion. But he knew he could not even try to make contact in case the ever-present NKVD traced him to them. They would suffer greatly, being relatives of a "traitor". He did not know that nearly five decades would have to pass before he would be reunited with the only surviving member of his family!

CHAPTER 7

England: Freedom, Family, Fellowship

The steamer docked at Dover on a cold, grey, February evening. Wasyl admired the legendary "white cliffs"; there was even an English castle nearby. The voyage had left Wasyl cramped and rather unsteady on his feet and, though on land, he could still feel the ocean swell.

It was time for another train journey, this time to London under the supervision of British officials. These men were nothing like the rough and arrogant commissars; they were welcoming and ready to converse. Wasyl could not believe how well appointed the train carriages were. After all, they were just ordinary rolling stock: fine seats, polished wood trimmings and windows with blinds! A far cry from the carriages he had travelled in before or those terrible cattle trucks...

On arrival in London, they were split into smaller groups and taken to one of the many hotels. If Wasyl was amazed by the appointments in the train, he was aghast at the trappings of this rather low tariff hotel. He sank into the soft seats and ran his hands over the carpet. But it was not until he stood outside the hotel and gazed at the cars, buses, and convivial people going about their business freely and independently, that he really understood how far he was removed from the Soviet communist scourge. Although evidence of the war lay all around him, a veil descended over the European theatre. It was not only a matter of geographical span, but also of distance in relation to culture and creed. For the first time in many, many years, he felt unthreatened!

The next day Wasyl and the other displaced persons were each given the grand sum of two English pounds! This really made Wasyl's day. Now he not only lived like a king, but he could spend like one. The London retailers were descended upon by the now "wealthy" refugees, who bought necessary items of clothing and food.

The Mines in Danby

From London, Wasyl was taken north by train to Danby and billeted with other displaced persons in disused military barracks. He began working in the mines, extracting iron ore for smelting. The work was quite different to what he expected. After a few weeks they worked in pairs, using drills as well as picks and shovels and laying the occasional explosive. Shifts were from 6 am to 2 pm, and from 2 pm to 10 pm. At the end of a gruelling week, he was paid the princely sum of £2/10/-. With his first pay packet, Wasyl went shopping and bought himself a shirt and pair of 'best' trousers. If this was capitalism, then it was very acceptable indeed!

He worked alongside a number of English miners and found them very friendly. One particular miner invited Wasyl and a Polish workmate to Sunday dinner. They were quite honoured at this invitation and speculated about what it would be like to be in an English home. When the appointed day arrived, they made their way to the house, an unpretentious brick dwelling in which the front door opened directly onto the footpath. Upon entering, they were introduced to the family and then escorted to the dinner table. Wasyl was again surprised to see how well these workers lived. These architecturally regimented miners' cottages were more than adequately appointed with separate rooms, comfortable furniture and tasteful furnishings. Democracy had even allowed these men a voice in government!

There were a few moments of uncomfortable silence as they were all a little unsure of each other, the hosts understandably apprehensive about how they would fit in. As for Wasyl and his fellow guest, well, they were bewildered! So many spoons, knives and forks! Which ones would they use? The Pole whispered to Wasyl, *"Don't touch anything until they do!"* Sensing their difficulty, their host showed them how to begin. There was so much food: meat, roast potatoes and a copious amount of vegetables. At the end of this hearty meal there was, of course, the traditional cup of tea. Conversation was very limited because of the language barrier, but there were enough smiles and nods to convey their appreciation to the family for their kindness. Wasyl never forgot it.

Mine explosion

One day in the mines, there was an explosion in a connecting shaft close to where Wasyl and a few others were digging. Rubble and dust hurled through on top of them. Two young Poles were killed and many miners injured. Wasyl was knocked unconscious and received a number of bruises and abrasions. He thought he had been in an air raid because of the wailing emergency sirens.

The next day they discovered that he had sustained a serious back injury and for two months he was unable work. Sickness benefits of thirty-two shillings and sixpence per week left him just two and sixpence for spending. Unfortunately, his back failed to heal sufficiently for him to return to the mines. What was he to do? He had a two year contract with the government to work as a miner. He suggested that he should be sent to Germany, as conditions there had improved since the American occupation. This was rejected because the government still wanted young men in industry, so they consigned him to a pottery mill near Nottingham, central England. However, the work there involved shovelling and barrowing clay, and was injurious to him. Eventually, he was assigned to painting canvas coverings for train carriages.

Towards the end of 1950, Wasyl was able to choose his own

employment. The railway was quite suitable, but he had heard of some young Ukrainian Christians gathering at Bradford. The Ukrainians in the church at Nottingham where he attended were older, and he felt he needed to mix with Christians of his own age. Collecting the little he had saved, he took a train to Bradford, hoping to locate these Christians and find another job.

Believers gathered unto the Lord - Nottingham UK - 1950s
(Wasyl fourth left front)

It was not long before enquiries led him to those he was seeking. They were very glad to see him and straightaway asked if he could play the piano and help them form a choir. Wasyl needed little encouragement; his musical skills were now in demand and he accepted their invitation enthusiastically. But where was he to stay and what about finding a job? Here again the Lord provided. Among these Christians there was a young man called *Mickey Kulikovsy,* who had been an evacuee in Europe. Unknown to Wasyl, he had travelled with his family along the same road as he had, fleeing communism and Hitler. Now, years later, they were again on the same road, a spiritual path, united in their faith. There was no question about it, Wasyl just had to come and stay with him and his family. Moreover,

Mickey could find Wasyl a job in one of the local woollen mills.

Mickey's family readily accepted Wasyl and he stayed with them until they both left, around September 1951. Both he and Mickey wanted to attend a Bible college. There was very little chance to learn the Word of God amongst the Ukrainians, as very few of them were able to read the English Christian literature. For their part, the English believers were willing teachers, but they had no understanding of Ukrainian or Russian. Wasyl and Mickey had heard of a Bible college in Swansea where foreigners were taught English as well as the Scriptures.

There was a problem however, the college was in Wales, and attendance required annual fees of £45. One Sunday, a Christian by the name of John Thomas, visited their meeting and, to their amazement asked, *"Who among you would like to go to a Bible college in Swansea?"* *"We would like to go but we have no money for the fees,"* said Wasyl. *"Don't worry,"* he said. *"Make your way there and allow the Lord to find your fees, leave all to Him."* So Wasyl and Mickey, after committing themselves to the Lord, set out for Swansea Bible College, raiding their paltry savings for the train tickets.

Swansea

The train journey to Swansea was enjoyable. They marvelled at the quaint railway stations and verdant countryside with its sleepy villages of thatched cottages and colourful gardens. In many ways it was an adventure, and an air of excitement attended them at the prospect of meeting fellow students and learning English and the Scriptures. On arrival at the station, they hired a taxi to take them directly to the Bible College. The driver stopped outside the main gate, set in a high, imposing, grey stone wall that surrounded the college buildings. Preferring a more discreet entrance, they walked through a side gate and found themselves near the kitchen.

No one appeared to be about, so they waited patiently, believing John Thomas would have informed someone to expect them. But no one came! Were they at the right place? Where were all the students? The sign said "Swansea Bible College"! They stood in anticipation, bags and coats in hand, for about twenty minutes.

Eventually a lady walked by and asked, *"Can I help you?" "We are new students,"* said Mickey. *"Do they know you are coming?"* she asked. Mickey said, *"John Thomas sent us." "Ah,"* she said, *"Well we know John Thomas, come with me and I will get someone to help you."* She led them to another building and disappeared inside. A few minutes later two students appeared, a Russian girl, *Marie*[62] and a young Ukrainian named *Nick*. They welcomed Wasyl and Mickey and after a brief conversation, Nick took them to their dormitories and then conducted them on an orientation of the college. There was quite a variety of nationalities among the students and boarders, including several Jews, rescued from under the very nose of Hitler.[63]

Mickey, Nick, Marie and Wasyl - students at Swansea Bible College

Later, Wasyl and Mickey went on a tour of Swansea, the second largest city in Wales, situated along its south-eastern coastal region. With coal and minerals in its hinterland, Swansea was a vital industrial port during the war and had been a major target for Hitler's Luftwaffe. This provincial city nestling beneath the rolling hills, sits along a relatively wide bay, its shoreline known for attractions such as Oyster Mouth castle and the (now defunct) Mumbles railway and pier.

The grounds of the Bible College overlooked the bay and on a sunny day the view was imposing. Wasyl remembered vividly the beauty of manicured lawns set against the pristine blue of the bay and the bright summer sky. He often made time to walk in the gardens, amongst the riot of variegated colour. The rhododendrons, roses, hydrangeas, daisies and camellias, all set in their appointed places, emitted a heady perfume. And there was an oak tree, larger than life itself, with a near five hundred years old heritage. The garden in summer was apt reminder of all things bright and beautiful, the very handiwork of the Creator Himself, One whom Wasyl had come here to know more about.

There was little time for recreation once the academic year began, as classes, domestic chores and devotions took up much of the day. Typically, each week-day began at an early hour, with each student allotted a task - gardening, kitchen duties or general maintenance. This lasted about an hour, and was followed by a communal breakfast and prayers. Formal lessons began at 10 am and lasted until lunch at 12.30 pm. After the hour-long midday meal, there was a little time for rest before classes again at 2 pm. Dinner was served at 5 pm, a session of private study followed and, finally, an evening prayer meeting between 7 pm and 8 pm closed the day. On Saturdays, each student had to do half a day's work in the morning and the afternoon was "free time", during which students visited local Christians, undertook additional study or just went for an outing. If venturing outside the college, it was mandatory for students to inform the staff where they were going and confirm their return before curfew.

Wasyl and Mickey often visited the Christians gathered to the Lord's name at Heol-O-Gors, FforestFach and Treboeth, especially on Sundays. The depth of sound teaching and Scriptural practice within these meetings played a significant part in the spiritual development and stability of both Wasyl and Mickey.

Wasyl settled into the routine of the college and buried himself in his studies, thoroughly enjoying the lessons from able teachers such as Ian Jones, Mr Samuel Howels, Dr Pridie, and Miss Scott, his English teacher, who had spent many years as a missionary in China.

One day, Wasyl was called into the college office and the young administrator asked coyly, *"Wasyl, do you know that your fees for the first and second terms have not been paid?"* Wasyl was taken aback for he thought John Thomas was arranging payment. *"No!"* replied Wasyl, *"I am sorry but I have no money to pay for the fees for the first, second or third terms. I thought they had already been paid!"* *"Don't worry,"* said the secretary, *"We will both pray for the fees to be paid somehow. You just set your mind on your studies and leave the rest with the Lord."*

About a week later, she called Wasyl to the office again, *"Good news Wasyl, your fees have all been paid and there is even something left over, £2!"* Wasyl found out that the money was sent by a Mr Lewis from the Slavic Gospel Association, and he wrote to him thanking him for his gift. Mr Lewis wrote back and hastened to inform Wasyl that it was not his gift. The money had been donated by a Christian man in Belfast, Ireland, who wished to remain anonymous. *"Just receive it as from the Lord,"* was Mr Lewis's reply.

It was a condition of enrolment at the college that

students had to live by faith, looking only to the Lord to supply their temporal needs. This was a discipline that stood Wasyl and all the students in good stead as servants of their Lord, even though Wasyl was not a stranger to it, for as a refugee he had had to depend on the providential hand of God in so many ways.

Swansea Bible College, Wales - Staff and students
(Wasyl second from end; Mickey, top middle)

Marriage

There was a young female student at the college whose presence had not gone unnoticed by Wasyl, despite the strict segregation between the sexes. In fact, we may say that the two took no small personal interest in each other. So it was that in 1955, Wasyl married Joy Morris, who was born and bred in Birmingham. Apart from their faith in Christ and fervent desire to serve Him, they had other things in common. Joy, like Wasyl, was from a large family, one which saw hard times during the Great Depression. She had lost her parents in her childhood and had been brought up unselfishly by her older sisters. Wasyl and Joy were married in London and it was through the kindness of Mr Schneidrook, a close Christian friend, that their wedding was arranged and paid for.

It was several years since Wasyl's arrival in England as an impoverished, lonely and homeless displaced person. Now his Lord had richly blessed him with a good education, a Christian wife, a home and a multitude of friends.

"I waited patently for the Lord;
And He inclined unto me, and heard my cry.
He brought me up also out of an horrible pit,
Out of the miry clay,
And He set my feet upon a rock,
And established my goings.
And He hath put a new song in my mouth,
Even praise unto our God:"

(Psalm 40: 1-3)

CHAPTER 8

Return to Europe

Europe - 1957

Wasyl became preoccupied about how he was to serve God. He had harboured a desire to return to Europe, for he had not forgotten his promise to the Lord to take His precious Word to a needy generation. Where and how was he to begin?

After looking to the Lord for guidance, he was able to return to Europe with the help of the Slavic Gospel Association and found himself working amongst the *lager camps* in Austria, Italy and Germany. These camps housed refugees and displaced persons, casualties of the war in Europe, even though the conflict had ended some twelve years before. Because of their old age or poor health, these displaced persons were refused citizenship into other countries. Europe had changed and Wasyl barely recognised Nurnberg and München. Sadly, he was unable to trace any of the Christians he had met prior to his departure for England.

There was much work to be done in the camps and Wasyl found himself involved in organising gospel meetings and helping with the many manual tasks. His knowledge of Russian, Ukrainian and German languages was put to good use among the camp populations and he felt he was where God intended him to be.

The gospel meetings were generally well attended with many gatherings held in the homes of missionaries. There were some within the camps who confessed faith in Christ, but there were also many "parcel professions", those who seemed to go through the motions in order to receive food

Gospel audience, displaced persons - Austria 1960s

packages. Furthermore, there was considerable resistance from the Catholic church in Austria and in Italy, where Protestants were regarded as heretics.

After about six weeks, Wasyl believed it was time to return to England and to his wife, Joy.

Birmingham 1957

Wasyl and Joy settled in Redditch, near Birmingham, living in a rented caravan on a dairy farm. During the week, Wasyl worked in a shop sorting and storing goods. On the weekends he took the gospel to Slavic speaking people who had settled in the area, basing his operations from the brethren assembly in Birmingham. Just before their two oldest children were born, the family rented a larger house in Smethwick. By then, Wasyl had secured work on the railways as a "tapper" (line examiner).

Europe 1958

The opportunity arose again for Wasyl to serve the Lord in Europe. He left his family in Birmingham and began working amongst the refugees, particularly in Austria and

Italy, organising gospel meetings and tract distributions. The response among the people was very mediocre, they had become hardened and had embraced materialism. However, the precious Seed was sown and the future will reveal the extent of the harvest!

After several months, Wasyl decided to return to Birmingham to spend time with his wife and children. How he thanked God for them! However, on his way home through Germany he was persuaded to remain in Europe by Slavic missionaries. Wasyl's commitment, experience and language skills were invaluable for the Lord's work there. In June 1958, the Christians arranged for Joy and the children to join Wasyl in Germany.

Austria

The family was led to Austria, initially settling in a tiny village not far from Spital, in the south-east, well positioned to reach Italy and Yugoslavia with the gospel. Their accommodation comprised two rented rooms above a farm house; one a large bedroom and the other a small kitchen. This proved rather inconvenient as the family was in continual receipt of guests, passing missionaries and locals in need. There was just insufficient room! Often, to accommodate visitors, the children had to give up their beds, sleeping in suitcases or cupboard drawers. Later, they were able to rent a larger home in *Pobersach*.

To stay in Austria for any appreciable period of time, foreigners had to have a regular income and disclaim all rights to social services. Initially, these problems were avoided by the family moving every three to four weeks between Austria, Italy and Yugoslavia, returning to Austria each time as visitors.

However, because of the birth of their third child and the ineffectiveness of such an itinerant life-style, the Slavic Gospel Mission came to their aid and gave them a monthly allowance of about $100US. This satisfied the Austrian authorities and they were allowed to stay. The allowance was used for running and maintaining their second-hand Volkswagen vehicle, Wasyl's workhorse for gospel trips into Italy and Yugoslavia. There was little money left for food, clothing and other expenses. Clothes were mostly home-made, supplemented by gifts from Christians in England. For food, they relied on their garden, and on food parcels from England and donations from local Christians.

The family settled into the routine of village life. Joy had become quite fluent in German, as had the children, who relished the joys of living in alpine climes - skiing and skating in winter, mountain walks and bathing in the cool lakes in summer. There were the occasional trips into Italy and to the markets in Trieste.

It was not long before Wasyl established a rapport with the local people, holding gospel meetings and distributing gospel literature in Spital, Arnoldstein, Klagenfurt and Villach. In addition to pastoral work, Joy held Scripture meetings for the women.

A Christian meeting in a little village in Austria, near Spital 1965
(Joy extreme right)

During this time, the family often worked with a number of Christian sisters from Holland, who also had been led to minister to the displaced persons and surrounding villages. They had set up operations nearby, and were frequent visitors. Their friendship and fellowship redounded to the glory of the Lord[64].

On occasions, Wasyl and the family would drive through Germany or Switzerland, then journey through either France or Holland, finally taking the ferry to England. The purpose of these trips was to stock up on Bibles, meet contacts, and report on the work in Europe.

Wasyl soon began regular visits into Romania, Yugoslavia, Italy and Greece, taking precious Bibles and gospel tracts with him. It was during this time that he met Dr Fred Tatford at one of the gospel and ministry weeks in a little village in Yugoslavia. Wasyl remembered the occasion well. Believers had gathered from Macedonia, Bosnia, Montenegro, and some even from Czechoslovakia. Some walked hundreds of kilometres, others came by a ferry plying the Danube, and a few came by motor car. These were times of great spiritual enrichment and resonant brotherliness. During the evenings, 200 to 300 believers packed a small hall to hear brethren minister the Word of God. Local Christians opened their homes to visitors, sharing liberally their food and accommodation. It was an opportune time to distribute Bibles!

Greece

Many Russian refugees had fled to Greece during the war and during the post-war purges of Stalin. Wasyl was determined to reach them also with the gospel, making several long trips to Athens itself. With the family's help, he would cram the VW Combie the night before departure with gifts for the refugees (clothes, food and other necessities), taking just enough provisions to sustain himself. These were long and lonely five to six day treks, driving through Italy, then taking a boat to Athens via

Corinth. On occasions, he went via communist Yugoslavia, a shorter journey, but quite dangerous.

The gospel was well received by the refugees and by many of the locals in Greece. He had made contact with a Christian Greek woman, who had married a Russian whilst living in the USSR. Her husband was still imprisoned under Stalin as a Greek spy. There was strong resistance to the gospel from the Greek Orthodox church and government officials. Often, orthodox priests infiltrated the gospel meetings. Wasyl did not mind, as it was good for them to hear the gospel. In some areas, the officials prohibited these meetings, thinking them to be communist-inspired. On one occasion, a sympathetic official advised Wasyl to conduct the meetings while serving food. This would create the impression of a "get-together" and not attract suspicion. It worked!

Romania

The authorities in this country were ardent communists, and meetings to preach the gospel were prohibited, but

A winter gospel meeting in a village cemetery - Romania

every opportunity was taken to proclaim the Word of God and distribute Bibles. This included funerals, which were permitted, providing of course there was no 'sermon'. However, Wasyl and other gospel preachers accompanied the funeral procession to the grave yard, and as they walked they sang hymns and declared how the deceased came to be a Christian! Of course, they ensured that the procession took the longest route to the grave site, and that it traversed the most populated streets of the village. At the grave itself, several eulogies were given to those assembled, all within earshot of surrounding houses. These funerals lasted between five to six hours, and provided a vital opportunity of declaring the gospel!

On other occasions, Christians gathered for the purpose of welcoming a 'good friend' who, of course, was Wasyl! They were permitted to hold 'festive' meetings, so long as the gospel was not proclaimed. However, at these meetings which were held in homes, accompanied by food and song, Wasyl would begin to speak about 'Paul', 'Peter' and 'John', friends whose greetings and messages he brought with him! Later, the authorities allowed just one meeting on Sundays which, needless to say, lasted the whole day!

Despite the repression, the Word of God was accomplishing that purpose to which it had been sent! Wasyl, and other missionaries with him, were much encouraged by the earnest desire of the Romanians to hear of the saving grace of God. The Christians would ride from village to village to inform of the arrival of Wasyl and the Bibles. One man hitched and rode a bicycle five hundred kilometres to Brashov to collect six small Bibles that Wasyl had smuggled in, in order to take them back to his village. The Bibles, wrapped in plastic and hidden in jars of gherkins, would augment the hand-written New Testaments shared between the villagers.

Yugoslavia

In the early 1960's, the Lord led Wasyl to concentrate

on taking the gospel into Yugoslavia, particularly Bosnia and Croatia. Taking Bibles into this region was hazardous. Although Tito, the then president, practised a moderate form of socialism, the USSR held the upper hand and any person caught taking in Bibles faced at least ten years imprisonment or could be tried as a Western spy. However, Tito, said Wasyl, was a good piano-player who could play equally well with his left or right hand, depending on the prevailing political stake! Wasyl had to be extra careful, because his defection from the Red Army was still open for prosecution. If he was caught and his history traced, he would be condemned to death or, at the very least, imprisoned for life!

Wasyl visited Yugoslavia about four times annually. The risks involved called for persistent prayer and careful planning. Several strategies were designed to minimise the chance of being apprehended. He would set out in the early hours of the morning, between midnight and 2 am, depending on the border crossing he selected, which in turn depended on weather and contacts. Border crossing points had to be alternated to avoid becoming known to the guards. Generally, Wasyl worked alone and without much "publicity", so as to diminish the chance of discovery and lessen the danger to other Christians.

The heavily laden Volkswagen Combie required gentle coaxing through the Alps, especially in the depths of winter (the most profitable time for evangelism). Although reliable, the motor was not entirely suited to the rugged terrain. Black ice and blinding snow were especially dangerous. Reaching the border check-points during the early hours generally ensured scant attention from the guards, who were either too sleepy or too warm beside their fire to conduct more than a cursory inspection. However, on one occasion, Wasyl was so early that he was the only one at the check-point for some time, and he came under close scrutiny. Their suspicion was aroused when the search revealed baby clothes which were intended as gifts. He was asked sarcastically, *"For you?!"* Continuing their search, they came across his squeeze-box accordion and sheet music, which they alleged were "secret papers". Wasyl took the

Willing workers parcel Bibles for smuggling into Yugoslavia and Romania

opportunity to introduce some music into the situation to lessen the tension and distract the guards from their search. Emboldened by the moment, he began playing "What a friend we have in Jesus...", followed by a robust version of "Come to the Saviour..." "*You seem to play quite a bit, play us some folk songs!*" said one of the guards. "*This instrument can only play religious music!*" retorted Wasyl jokingly. The ruse had worked, for by this time several other vehicles had arrived, and the searching of Wasyl's van was cut short, leaving the Bibles undiscovered.

Wasyl recounted many close encounters with the border guards, even one alarming occasion when the Bibles were discovered. Providentially, he and his precious cargo were permitted to continue into Yugoslavia, but only after the guard insisted on receiving his own copy of the sacred volume.

During the 1960's, Wasyl continued to take Bibles into socialist Yugoslavia and other neighbouring Iron Curtain countries. On each visit he would meet and encourage the local believers in their worship and service in the gospel of Christ. However, the door began to close as political and domestic circumstances altered. The KGB became an increasing danger. Wasyl and his family then returned to England, serving the Lord within South Wales and Devon.

CHAPTER 9

Australia: Bibles by Mail Order

While in England, Wasyl had little opportunity to witness to his Slavic brethren, apart from occasional visits into the Eastern Bloc. He heard that there were increasing numbers of his countrymen escaping or emmigrating to Australia from the Continent, many of them yet to be reached with the gospel of Christ. So, after months of prayer, and with the commendation from their brethren in Wales, the family set sail on the *Britanis* for Australia. One month later, having docked in Spain and in Cape Town in South Africa, they arrived in Melbourne.

It was as he expected! There was a large contingent of Slavic people in Melbourne, among whom he was able to preach the message of salvation. He and other Slavic Christians continued to exhort the unsaved and, over the years, led many of their countrymen and others to accept Christ as their Lord and Saviour[65]. Apart from ministering the gospel from the pulpit and personal evangelism, Wasyl translated Christian literature into the Slavic tongue, in order to expose his people to Christian teaching.

Bibles behind the Iron Curtain
Despite the challenging and rewarding work among the Slavic people in Australia, Wasyl had an abiding concern for his countrymen still fettered under socialism. He yearned to bring to them the gospel of Christ, but how was he to achieve this?

In 1989, through a contact in Germany, he became aware of some Ukrainians who were in need of Bibles.

The Slavic Gospel Association in Australia gave him some Ukrainian Bibles, which he sent to the Ukraine. The chance of these Bibles reaching their destination was, to say the least, very slight. Much prayer accompanied their journey and they did arrive safely, as testified to by the letters of thanks he received.

There was another letter that arrived some time after these letters of thanks! This one was to mark the continuation of an extensive distribution of Bibles into the Ukraine. The following is a translated extract from that letter:

"Dear Countryman,

I hope you do not think me bold. I was at our village post office the day your parcel of Christian literature arrived. The person to whom it was sent told me that you had sent them a Bible. I got your address from the parcel and now I am writing to please request one for myself! I do not know you, and you are from a far-away country. But, I pray that you will be able to send me a Bible too! I want to learn more about God, and learn how to pray to Him. Bibles are hard to get and those that are available are too costly for the people to buy!"

The arrival of this letter was cause for thanksgiving and set a challenge! Wasyl set about sending this man a Bible. Here was a real need, one he identified with through his own life's experience.

However, Wasyl was not prepared for what followed. Over the subsequent months, dozens of requests for Bibles and Christian literature poured in each month from the Ukraine. The country had, as we know, undergone a political change which enhanced religious freedom. The people, who for so many years had been spiritually starved under the barren regime of communism, were now making an urgent enquiry about God and Christianity. The requests tell of this fervour, as seen through the following translated letters and extracts.

Request - 9/10/1990
"I am Waldamir _____. I am in the 7th class in school. My sister Tanya, she is in the 5th class. My elder brother Nicoli is in technical school. Till last year, we were never allowed to go to church and we were never allowed to talk about God in school. Now it is different. Our teacher started to pray before school each day and we can go to church. I know very little about God, but I want to know more. In our school, I got your address and they said you send Bibles. Can you send me one and other Christian books so I can know who God is!"

Request - Maria, September, 1990
"My name is Maria, I have two children. Each Sunday we go to church to hear about God, but it is not enough for us. Our neighbour received a parcel from you of Christian books. My children and I would like some for our reading at home...".

Request - village regional library (Biblioteka)
"I am a Christian in the Ukraine and have a big request! Please send me a Bible and Christian literature as much as possible for our village library. In our village school they are now teaching about God. But there are no Christian books in the library. Children and teachers come and ask to borrow these books, but we have none. We want our village children to know more about God....."

The reply from the village regional library
"Dear Sir,

Our library received your parcel of Christian books. They are now in our library and many come in to read them, teachers, primary students, university students and 'big' people. We want to thank you for such a great gift."

Request - *Maria, 3/4/1991*

"Man of good deeds,

I am a teacher in the Ukraine. Now in our schools we can teach about God, and we need to teach children about Him. I am keen to teach them, but I do not have a Bible. I got your address from some others who received a Bible from you and I have a great request. This Holy Book, send one to me to learn and teach from. I shall be very glad if you can do this. I shall pray the Lord bless you. I and the children will be glad."

Reply - *Maria, 27/11/1991*

"Dear Mr Boltwin,

I want to thank you for the parcel you sent me. I received all in good condition. As you notified me in your letter, nothing has been omitted. Now, I can read the Bible to my students and bring them to a knowledge of God. I am thankful of your advice how to study the Bible for myself."

Request - *Wasyl, 24/4/1990*

"Our dear countryman,

I came to know about you from some others who received a Bible from you. I wish you could possibly send me one too. Our people started turning back to God. I am now an old man and would like to read about God in my old age and teach my children and grandchildren about God. In our country it is impossible for people like us to get such a Book."

Request - *Vasilli*

"Dear Sir,

I apologise from the bottom of my heart that I trouble you with this letter, because you don't know me and I you. Not long ago, I went to the post office and saw a schoolboy from our village receive a parcel from a far country, Australia. I have lived here for 55 years and this was the first time I have seen a Bible. Do not be amazed at that. I write to you because I lived in a land called once a socialist educated land. They tried to suppress and destroy all religion. They told us it was opium for the people. But all things in life come and go, people started now to learn about God and are happier because now they can praise God and read Christian books.

There are not enough of such books here and it is impossible for people like us to get them. I have the courage to ask you, because at my age, I want to know about God. I have never seen let alone possess a Bible. Please forgive my boldness, a schoolboy gave me your address."

Request - *Anna, Natalie, Garla, Wasyl, Tania, Erika and Ivan*

"Dear Christian,

We are children who believe in God.......in our country it is impossible for us to get Bibles, please understand us and help us. We know the main thing in life is to have faith, but we do not know where to draw from."

Request - *Walter 16/2/1990*

"I am the father of two children, who always ask me about the Lord Jesus Christ. However, I too am ignorant about the Lord. I would like to tell my children. Please will you send me a Bible.....?"

From 1989 to 1994 there were over 500 letters, from mothers, grandmothers, fathers and grandfathers, children, students and even from Orthodox priests, requesting Bibles and Christian literature! Today, throughout the Ukraine, there are homes, schools, churches and public libraries which contain Bibles sent by Wasyl, their dispersion generously assisted by the freewill donations from Christians in Australia!

The Lord has graciously enabled Wasyl to keep his promise to Him, made so many years earlier in times of great danger and destitution! And, here, in closing this little volume, it is needful and fitting to pay tribute to the many fervent and courageous souls, who over the years, have sought to plant and preserve the Word of God within hostile territory.

Profane history is replete with man's efforts to eradicate God's Word. All such efforts have failed and will always fail, because the righteousness of God and the work of God can never be extinguished!

Epilogue

In 1994, through the grace of God, Wasyl was able to fulfil a cherished desire. He and his wife returned to England to visit the many Christians they had come to know and work with in past years. Following his reunion with his sister Natasha in 1990, and despite failing health, Wasyl was able to journey to Germany where he met a niece and her family. He was thrilled to know that her parents were part of the underground church during the communist oppression.

Simon's whereabouts had been unknown, but Wasyl was able to trace him in Germany. The long search had left him just enough time to make telephone contact. It was then he came to know why God had led him away from the little village of Novomyrovka in the forest at the end of 1943. Up to that day, he had wondered why he was not destined to stay with the Christians there! Just a few months after Wasyl had left that little village, the Red Army arrived. Trofim, his wife Maria, and yes, little Mary also, were, with the other Christians, shot as collaborators![66]

Simon had returned to the village after liberation, only to find it occupied by the communists! Wasyl despaired as Simon told him of the fate of the Christians in the village. No wonder Wasyl could not trace them. However, his consolation was that he knew little Mary, and the others, were now with their Lord. He remembered her words by the fire over fifty years ago in that snow-shrouded forest cottage concerning her deceased parents, words which then had so bewildered him - *"But I will see them again!"* Wasyl had been brought to realise once again, that he had been **saved to serve!**

Let us all, who have been saved by the grace of God through the cross work of His beloved Son redeem the time in His service, for all of us who have been saved by Him, have been **saved to serve!**

> *"...thanks be to God, which giveth us*
> *the victory through our Lord Jesus Christ.*
> *Therefore, my beloved brethren,*
> *be ye stedfast, unmoveable,*
> *always abounding in the work of the Lord,*
> *forasmuch as ye know that your labour*
> *is not in vain in the Lord."*
> *(1 Corinthians 15.57-58)*

Footnotes

[1] Psalm 36:5

[2] Psalm 31:15

[3] *Stal* means *steel*; *Stalin*, "*man of steel*".

[4] "*Victory of the Counter-Revolution in Vienna*" 1848 (Quoted in "*A Farewell to Marx, An Outline and Appraisal of his Theories*"; D Conway, Pelican,1987).

[5] *ibid,*. K Marx, (Editorial in Neue Rheinische Zeitung No. 301, 1849).

[6] Luke 6:45

[7] Not to be confused with the "Great Terror" of 1936 to 1938.

[8] During the revolutionary period, they were called the "Cheka", then the GPU (1922-23), the OGPU (1923-34) and the NKVD (1934-43). Later on they were referred to as the NKGB, the MGB and MVD. We knew them as the infamous KGB during the Cold War.

[9] Lenin: "*The Man Behind The Mask*", R W Clark, Faber and Faber, page 377, August 4th 1920, *Pravda* (Truth), the voice of the Communist Party.

[10] Psalm 111:10

[11] Psalm 36:1-2; Proverbs 14:34

[12] J S Mill "*Three Essays*"

[13] D F Strauss (Higher Critic 1808-1874)

[14] John 1:17

[15] Some time later, Wasyl learned that his friend Metji's mother was a Christian. He remembered she behaved differently to the other women on the collective farm in Belgrad. She never swore or drank vodka and did not participate in the communist meetings on the farm. After being "relocated" she fell from a building and died. Many Christians during that time fell from buildings!

[16] Many captured Russian soldiers who went home after being liberated were branded as traitors. Some had suffered in Hitler's concentration camps. On return to Russia, they were executed or sent to Stalin's lags as defectors or subversives.

[17] Romans 10:9

[18] Philippians 2:11

[19] I Corinthians 12:3

[20] 1 Corinthians 15:55

[21] 1 Corinthians 11:3-16

[22] Revelation 1:6 (Rendering the debate over male and female priests entirely irrelevant!).

[23] 1 Peter 2:5

[24] Hebrews 13:15 (Bearing in mind of course, the injunction regarding audible expression from the women within the church, in 1 Timothy 2:11-14 etc.)

[25] 1 Peter 2:9

[26] 1 Peter 2:9

[27] Hebrews 10:21-22

[28] Matthew 18:20

[29] Matthew 18:20

[30] 2 Peter 1:16, Revelation 1, 4, 5

[31] Acts 24:25

[32] Acts 17:30, Psalms 9:16, 2 Peter 3:9

[33] Romans 5:19

[34] Romans 3:10 & Romans 5

[35] Psalm 119:89

[36] Psalm 119:11, Romans 5:19

[37] Romans 3:23

[38] 1 Corinthians 1:25

[39] Isaiah 64:6

[40] Ephesians 2:8

[41] Galatians 2:16

[42] 2 Corinthians 5:21

[43] Psalm 19:1

[44] John 14:6

[45] Luke 15:18

[46] Luke 18:9-14

[47] Matthew 9:13

[48] 2 Thessalonians 1:9; Revelation 20:10

[49] The agnostic rationalists Diderot and Voltaire, believed in a place beyond the grave where unremitted sins on earth are judged.

[50] John 3:16-18

[51] Romans 4:25

[52] Romans 5:1

[53] John 14:1-3. The present reality, is that He will be where we *are*. (Matt 18:20) . In a coming day, we will be where He *is*!

[54] John 10:11

[55] Hebrews 13:5

[56] John 1:12

[57] 1 Corinthians 15:47

[58] John 3:1-18

[59] Isaiah 59:1

[60] Acts 8:36-39

[61] Luke 6:46

[62] Marie's father was a Christian missionary in Berlin who was taken captive by the Russians after the division of Berlin into East and West sectors. His fate is unknown. His crime was to receive food parcels from Christians in the United States - he was accused of espionage.

[63] Wasyl remembered one of these children well, a young Jewish boy named Hans who helped him learn English. Hans was an extremely intelligent boy whose parents were taken to a concentration camp. The college was also host to Lidj Asrate Kasse, the son of a relative of the Emperor, Haile Selassie, who visited the college.

[64] These sisters in the Faith, who live by faith, still continue their work for the Lord at the "*Holländische Mission*", Müllnern, Austria. Although some have "retired", others have taken their place.

[65] Mickey had also migrated to Australia and settled with his family in Adelaide, enabling him to continue his life-long fellowship in the gospel with Wasyl and his family.

[66] Simon was called home to be with the Lord in 1998. He was to his last days serving Him.